Freedom from Addiction

EXPERIENCING THE *SHIFT*

BOOK ONE

BONNIE BARNESS

DISCLAIMER: The information provided in this book is for entertainment purposes only. The author bears no responsibility for any consequences resulting from the use of this information. Please use all information at your own risk. Consult with a medical doctor and mental health provider. No part of this publication may be reproduced or transmitted in any form without the express permission of the author.

Copyright@ 2024 Bonnie Barness. All rights reserved.

Contents

A Note From The Author 4

Starting on YOUR NEW PATH 5

Step 1 *Knowing* YOU WANT MORE 7

Step 2 MAKING THE DECISION 19
TO DO *Whatever* IT TAKES

Step 3 PREPARING FOR YOUR 23
Upcoming Journey

Step 4 THE MAGICAL PLACE 31
of *Awareness*

ABOUT *the Author* 161

A Note from the Author

Dear Authentic You!

I am so excited to be with you as your start on your new path. Until now, you have been on a journey, the journey of life. Today, right now, you are about to step onto a new path. One that will lead to a new way of thinking, seeing and being in the world. You will discover who you truly are and begin manifesting dreams in a way you never believed possible.

All that you have experienced on your journey until now has led you to this moment, the moment in time when you will gain knowledge and wisdom that has alluded you. You will begin to release pain from the past, experiencing healing and a lightness of being.

On your new path, you will become aware of great Truths previously unseen. In the past, you may have wondered why the knowledge you had accumulated did not lead to the joy and happiness desired. I have created a process, *SHIFT* Actualization™, which utilizes ancient wisdom and modern knowledge to create a *SHIFT*, a *SHIFT* in conscious awareness, an awakening. Possibilities unseen before become potential realities. Life around you may be the same, but your experience of yourself and others is altered as you transcend to a higher vantage point that is as profound as it is powerful.

I am grateful and honored to be able to walk together by your side on this new path, sharing what I have been given that has allowed me to Experience the SHIFT and to experience additional ones throughout my life.

Wishing you much joy, peace and love on your amazing adventure!

Starting on Your New Path

STEP 1

Welcome onto your new path! I am so excited to take the next steps together with you as you begin your journey towards the happiness and joy you desire with all of your heart and soul. Without realizing it, you have already taken the first step on your new adventure. You did it when you opened this book.

The first step on your new path is connecting with the deepest part of your being. When you connected with the yearning to have more in your life and to be free from the heart-breaking effects of addiction, internally and externally, you connected with your True Self. The feeling and thoughts of wanting more led you to this moment.

Yay! You have just started on your journey. You have taken the first step on your new path. You listened when, from within, came the words, "I want more. I want to be free from addiction and the control that it has over my life." You connected with your emotional desire, your inner experience of desire, the desire for more. It is the combination of the desire and thought that has propelled you to take your first step.

Knowing that you want more from life and more for yourself has created the momentum to take the first step onto your new path. You may have taken this step as you walked into your home last night after another empty night of sex or when you were sick from all the food you ate. You may have stepped onto your new path last week as you wished your kids a great day when you dropped them off at school, all the time thinking about where you were going to get another pack of cigarettes or your next fix.

You may have taken it when entering the boardroom for a meeting or your classroom full of students, absorbed with thoughts about the credit card bill in your briefcase listing charges from your last visit to the casino. It may have happened as you saw the pain and disappointment in the eyes of a loved one or when crying in your room alone while pouring a drink. You may be taking it at this very moment.

Taking this first step is an affirmation. It is an affirmation of yourself. It is an affirmation of your desire to be free from the inner pain and to feel truly alive. You have begun a journey into the unknown. You have taken the first step on your new path. This first step comes from a place deep within. It comes from your heart and from your soul. The words, your thoughts, asserting themselves to be heard, saying, "I want more. I want more happiness. I want more fulfillment. Is this all there is? There must be more to life than this."

There may be questioning words filled with pain. "Why is happiness eluding me? Why is there so much conflict in my relationship? Why are my children so angry with me? Why haven't I been able to make some of my dreams come true? Why can't I stop smoking, using, drinking, over-eating, getting into unhealthy relationships, gambling, smoking weed, being angry, being sad, feeling anxious? What's wrong with me?" There are words crying out. "I didn't think my life would turn out like this. Why? Is this all there is? The pain of disappointment is too great. I can't take the pain any longer."

As heart wrenching as these words and thoughts are, they are actually a gift to you. It is your innermost self, your True Self, expressing its longing for more. From deep within, you hear yourself, your authentic voice, expressing a desire, a deep longing, to no longer suffer. It is calling out for more fun, excitement and passion. It wants to be heard. It needs to be heard.

You have been on your journey, your journey of life. You are now starting on a new path. As you step onto this new path, you are tapping into your desire to want more. You are tapping into your desire to be free from the control that addiction has had over you, your relationships and your life. With this step, change has been put into motion. Your emotion, the deep desire from within, is providing the energy you need to move forward with your new life and to take this first step. The first step to creating change comes from the desire to create something different. It comes from the desire to want more.

As a psychotherapist, I often see individuals who come to me in a lot of pain. They tell me, "I can't take it any longer." Others come because they are in a relationship with someone they love or are not sure if they still love, and don't want to continue to suffer. They are confused and do not know what to do. They want a close, happy relationship and don't know if they will ever have one.

Other people come to me because their life is out of control and they feel that they are out of control. They are filled with self-loathing and despair, yet, still having a tiny ray of hope in their heart. There are still others that come because they are happy, but want more from life, but don't know how to access it. They all took the first step acting on their desire to create change as you are now.

Take a moment and visualize yourself actually on your new path. Closes your eyes. What do you see? What does your path look like? Is it a dirt path? Does it look like a country road with a white picket fence on either side going forward further than your eyes can see? Is it a path made up of jewels shining and glittering in the light? Imagine taking your first step onto your path. What are you experiencing? Are you excited? Do you feel trepidation? Are you afraid, apprehensive? Now open your eyes and know that you are truly on your new path and that I am here by your side.

Often, when individuals start on their new path, they feel a lot of different emotions. One of the emotions that often comes up is fear. Fear that no matter what they will do, they will never be able to have all of the good things in life they see others have. Fear they will never be able to achieve their heart's desire. Fear of never being free of the hold addiction has over them and their life, having tried over and over again without attaining this elusive dream. Fear there is something inherently wrong with them and, somehow, undeserving of having their dreams become a reality.

Some people are afraid to try because they are afraid to fail, believing failure will be a confirmation of what they always feared to be true about who they are and their ability to have their dream come true, to be free of addiction. They are afraid of the shame and humiliation they are certain will be felt when others see them fail. Some people are afraid to go after their dreams because they believe it will confirm others' negative judgment of who they are. They are afraid they will then have to accept that they are "nothing special" or are simply "expecting too much from life."

Others are afraid to "rock the boat," concerned that when they begin to grow and change, conflict will occur in their relationships. Others are afraid to start on their new path, having an inner sense they will no longer want to be in their present unhealthy relationship or chosen career.

Still others may feel doubtful. Having shared their desire to have a healthier relationship with people in their lives or having asked for more of what they want, they have been told, "Oh, you're crazy," "You're selfish," or "You don't know what you are talking about," "You're just drunk," "Why would you want more? Be grateful for what you have."

Others have been made to feel that there is something wrong with them. Having heard repeatedly, "Why aren't you married?" "Why aren't you more successful?" "You're just an addict," "You won't amount to anything." They have begun to think that maybe what others have been saying has been correct all along. Feelings of hopelessness and powerlessness grow stronger day after day.

I am here to tell you that you can have more. You can transform your life. There is a way out of your internal and external pain and suffering and from all the "drama" in your life. There are higher heights to reach. You can have the peace and joy you have been wishing for in the deepest recesses of your being.

The first step is to feel the desire that is burning in your heart that hasn't been extinguished, even with everything you have been through over the years. It is this desire that is going to be the fuel you will be tapping into in order to create the changes you want in your life. The first step involves getting in touch with yourself, your thoughts, and your desires, allowing yourself to feel that which is so powerfully within, your longing to have more.

Acknowledge this wish and hear yourself say aloud, "I want to be in a happy and healthy relationship. I want to be successful. I want to like myself. I want to feel greater joy. I want a close relationship with my spouse. I want clarity. I want peace. I want to feel good about myself. I want to be good to myself. I want to have a sense of being in control of my life and my actions. I want to live free from fear, guilt, depression, anxiety and addiction. I want to live in passion."

Many people look at past and present self-destructive, unhealthy choices and their consequences, and get so weighed down by them that they feel they can never get out from underneath. If this is how you are feeling, know that you can and already have taken the first step to do so. Know that if you do not take the next steps, things will most likely stay as they are or may even get worse. Life is not stagnant. It is about change.

This book is a guide on how to have more in life. It is about taking control of your life. It takes courage to walk this path. You have taken the first step of your journey. It's about taking one step at a time. I will be with you as you take one after the other.

With each step you will gain hope and will begin to see change, first within yourself and then in your life. With each new step, you will begin to believe that you can have the greater happiness and peace that you desire because, with each step you actually will begin to experience these feelings.

Dr. Martin Luther King, Jr. said, "Take the first step in faith. You don't have to see the whole staircase. Just take the first step." This is your first step. You have taken it because from the depth of your being you still have hope that good things are yours to be had, greater heights can be reached.

Even though you do not know how you are going to attain this new way of being, deep within, you do have a belief in yourself and in the goodness of life, even after all you have been through. If you did not, you would have never opened up this book. You have already tapped into this belief and into your desire. You have taken the first step.

Remember, today, truly, is the first day of the rest of your life. Your journey has brought you to this moment in time. You have pulled from an inner source of power in order to begin on your new path and are now ready to take the next step.

Often, as the first step is taken, strong emotions arise. You may feel great excitement about the possibility of reaching ever higher heights of joy and depths of meaning. It is extremely important to let yourself feel whatever is coming up for you. If tears rise up from within, let them flow. Do not suppress the emotions that want to come out. Allow yourself to express these emotions. It is good to do so.

Allow yourself to release the pain that you have been holding inside yourself for such a long time. It is the pain that comes from trying, yet seeing nothing ever change. It is the pain of knowing there is more, but not knowing how to create it. It is the release of this pain which lets in more hope. It is good. It comes from the connection to yourself and the belief you are worthy of all the joy life has to offer.

Releasing the pain and sadness will make room for the light of hope to ignite in your heart and soul. You will find that, over time, in the place of tears, you will have a sparkle in your eyes. It is the light of hope, that maybe, just maybe, it is actually possible to live in a different way. Now is the time to start letting out the feelings of powerlessness and allowing yourself to feel hope as the kernels of optimism begin to emerge.

We all have a lot of pain that is held within, some we are aware of and some we are not. If you want to talk about what you are feeling with someone you trust, then let yourself be comforted. Allow yourself to receive the love and support that is here waiting for you. Or you can comfort and hug yourself, or write or draw in your journal if that feels good to you. Perhaps go to the gym or go for a walk and breathe in deeply of all the beauty that surrounds you.

Be alone or be with others. Do whatever is healthy and supports your happiness. Allow yourself to express the sadness you have carried for so long, so it can begin to be released. Feel the relief. Allow the excitement and hope to well up and propel you to take the next step on your new path. You have now taken your first step, connected with your desire to experience more joy and passion. You have asserted your desire to have more in life, to be free of addiction, to feel better. You are on your way. The next step is right in front of you. Are you ready? Here we go!

MAKING THE DECISION TO DO *Whatever* IT TAKES
STEP 2

All creation begins with a thought, followed by desire, and then is manifested through action. With your first step, you listened to your thoughts and got in touch with your desire to create change in your life and to become free from addiction. In order to make that desire a reality, the next step is essential. This step entails making the decision to take action. It requires a commitment to yourself to do whatever is necessary to create change and to transform your life.

You already have said, "I want more." Now, it's time to say, "I will do whatever it takes to be happy. It's up to me! I'm not going to let anyone or anything get in my way or stop me!" It's about being determined to take action to create the life you want. By making this decision you are asserting to yourself that you are no longer willing to be unhappy or to settle for "just okay." You are making a promise to yourself to do what is necessary to create positive change in your life. You are making a decision, choosing to go after what you want.

The decision comes from your desire, not from what you think you should do, but instead, from what you want to do. By choosing to do whatever it takes, you are making the decision to go after your happiness.

You are making the decision that you are no longer willing to hurt yourself or allow others to hurt you. You are making the decision to open yourself to new ideas and new ways of being in the world. You are making the decision to not just "get by." Making the decision to do whatever it takes is choosing to create a life filled with peace, passion, and fun.

We have all had painful experiences in our past that have wounded us. The pains from these wounds are often still present in us today. They can exert a powerful influence on our internal and external life.

Though we often did not have the ability in the past to prevent the wounding, we do have the ability now to free ourselves from the pain we still carry within. By making the decision to do whatever it takes to be happy, you are choosing to heal from the past so that you can experience more joy and move forward towards your dreams.

At the time of the wounding, you did not have the knowledge or ability to prevent the pain. You felt helpless and powerless. As you continue to move forward on your new path, you will begin to recognize your own power. Instead of feeling helpless, as you may have felt in your childhood or even yesterday, you will begin to realize that right now, today, you have the ability to tap into your inner source of power.

In this very moment, right now, you can make the decision to take control of your life and your happiness. By taking this step, you are reconnecting to the strength you have always had, but have become disconnected from.

You are a truly magnificent being with unlimited potential and beauty. Making this decision is acknowledging that Truth. You are allowing yourself to believe it might actually be so. Taking this next step is the action that YOU have decided to take. With this step, you are asserting your deep inner belief in yourself.

Choosing to move forward is choosing to *SHIFT* your focus from your past to the present and into your future. It is not about suppressing the pain or forgetting your past. Rather, you are choosing to act on your desire for more. It is about taking your life back into your own hands. It is about going after your dreams while letting go of the sadness inside related to some dreams that may not have been achieved in the past. It is about looking forward to the inner joy and happiness that awaits you.

By taking this step, you are choosing to see yourself as the unique and special person that you truly are and letting go of the negative views that you may have been holding or that others have imposed on you. You are choosing to use all the strength and determination you drew upon to survive to now create a wonderful present and future. It's up to you. It is your choice to make.

Life is waiting for you. Are you ready to grasp it and live it to its fullest? Now is your time. This is YOUR decision to make. Once taken, you will be on your way. Have you made the decision to do whatever it takes to feel great about yourself and to go after the life that you want and deserve?

PREPARING FOR YOUR *Upcoming* JOURNEY
STEP 3

Congratulations! You did it! You made the decision to go after what you truly desire, freedom from addiction. You have taken the second step and are ready to prepare for the next part of your journey. Now that you are in touch with your heart's desire and have made the decision to take whatever action is necessary to obtain it, you are ready for the next step. You ask, "How do I begin? What do I need to do to continue on my new path?"

As in any exciting adventure, there are preparations to be made. The time has arrived to put your desire and decision into action. Action is required to prepare for this wondrous and unique journey. You will require, two maps - a roadmap and a navigational map, a journal and special pen, and, lastly, your own personal Support Team, in order to reach your destination. To get ready to embark, it is now time to gather together everything necessary for the next steps of your journey.

Now, visualize yourself on the wondrous path you previously discovered, stretching ahead farther than your eyes can see. Notice how wonderful you feel. Now, look down. You see that you are holding a book in your right hand. As you look more closely, you realize that it is Freedom From Addiction: Experiencing The *SHIFT*, written by Bonnie Barness, the roadmap to your ultimate destination of joy and peace.

From the corner of your eye, you observe something on the ground and decide to take a closer look. As you walk over and bend down, you find a toolbelt. You wonder what is its purpose. You pick it up and try it on. Lo and behold, it is a perfect fit. As you place it around your hips, you are astonished at how comfortable it is. To your amazement, it actually feels as light as a feather. You examine it a bit more closely and observe a number of different-shaped pockets. One appears to have something in it.

You want to see what it could be, but decide to first find a pocket for the roadmap. Laughing with delight, you discover one made to the exact specifications required. After placing the new tool into its special pocket, you turn your attention to the object in your toolbelt. It appears to be some sort of scroll.

It looks very delicate, even ancient. Gently removing it, you walk over to a large rock nearby. Carefully, you begin to unroll this delicate scroll. Taking a closer look, you realize it is some sort of map, oh, a navigational map for your journey. Just as in a holographic image, the path you are on appears and there you are, sitting on the rock with the scroll in your hands! There is something red in the image, but you can't quite make it out. You think, "Hmmm. What could it be?"

As much as you want to spend more time looking at the map to find out what is to come, you decide to put it back on your toolbelt, excited to use it on your upcoming journey. Still a bit stunned and amazed by what was revealed within, you stand up, placing it carefully into the narrow, perfectly fitted opening. How are you feeling as it slides into place? Are you starting to sense that you really are preparing for the journey of your lifetime?

Hey, look over there. It looks like some sort of notebook. You walk over and pick it up. It is a special journal, The Experiencing the *SHIFT* Journal, with your name engraved on it and a beautiful pen attached to its side. You can see the place for it in your toolbelt. It slides smoothly into its designated pocket.

You're amazed how light everything feels. You notice a distinct feeling of being a bit more grounded, connected to the earth, realizing that somehow the toolbelt and what it contains is providing a wonderful sense of security.

Suddenly, you become aware of a powerful energetic vibration moving throughout your entire body. The excitement is almost impossible to contain. With your toolbelt and supplies, you know you are getting close to moving onto the next step of your new journey. But wait, what is it that you hear? It sounds like people talking and laughing. At first you cannot see them. Then, figures appear as a blur. They seem to be walking towards you and your path.

As they get closer, everything becomes more in focus. To your surprise, you see some friends and family members. You may, even, recognize a spiritual leader you know, a therapist or doctor you have met with, or maybe it's your golf buddies, the girls from Mahjong, a member of your book club or hiking group.

You may see people from AA or congregants

from your church or synagogue, or members of a therapeutic support group at the local neighborhood clinic. These are people that want to walk with you on your path in order to provide the support you may want and need.

Know that this is YOUR new path. You are just starting out on your own unique journey, beginning a completely new volume in the story of your incredible life. The steps you have already taken have prepared you for the upcoming journey. You have received some necessary tools and now you are making the choice as to who you would like to have as support during the first leg of your new adventure.

Look around and take some time to determine who you want to have join you at this time. Those selected are going to become part of your Support Team. There are lots of people to choose from. Some you know and others you have not yet met. You get to choose who will comprise your Support Team. Everyone present wants to be a support to you.

It is important not to feel that you SHOULD have someone on your Support Team because they want to be on it. Choose carefully. The essential qualifications of their participation are 1) you feel comfortable with them, 2) they are positive, 3) they are supportive and 4) they have what you will want and need, right now, for the first part of your journey. You know you definitely will choose a doctor, with the specific area of expertise you are addressing, to be a part of your Support Team.

As you look around more closely, now is the time to choose. Will it be a particular friend, family member or spiritual advisor. Oh, there's an Intuitive *SHIFT* AP™ Coach and Hypnotherapist who looks excited about the new path you are on. Choose your Support Team wisely. You may want to start with one or two members and then add others as you take a few more steps on your path.

As you move forward, you may find yourself in need of legal, financial, or educational support. You can always add new members to your Support Team with the specific expertise, knowledge and know-how desired at the time or needed going forward. You may even choose to take a class or sign-up for a program if you wish. If you have made the choice to become free from drugs or alcohol, finding a hospital where you can detox could be extremely beneficial.

As you determine who will be part of your team right now, know quality, not quantity is what matters. You and one other person may be what is best for the upcoming steps on your new path. Whatever you need, it is for you to discover and bring in. Remember, this is your sacred journey.

To your right, you notice that there is another group of people. You do not recognize anyone in this group. One of the individuals comes up to you and introduces herself. She tells you that she is actually on her own new path and is now free from her previous addictions since having experienced the *SHIFT*. She tells you that the people with her have experienced it as well. She reaches out her hand to you and lightly touches your arm, letting you know they would each be honored to be part of your Support Team.

You realize that the support they are offering will be of great service to you as you move ahead on this unknown path. You thank her and express that you are looking forward to having them come along. She smiles and goes back to share the great news with the other individuals in the group. As she does so, you feel a bit of relief knowing that you can learn from the experiences and knowledge they have gained from their own personal journeys. You also wonder how and when you will meet up with these new Support Team members again.

Returning to the task at hand, know you may choose not to bring in anyone else quite yet. Now is the time to make your decision. Think deeply and honestly, and if you would like to have one or more Support Team member, make your selection now. Great! You did it. You sense that the people you have chosen will play a very important role in your new adventure. Know that I am on your team too! With your Support Team in place, you now have everything needed for the next step of your journey.

You are prepared with your toolbelt and tools it contains comfortably and effortlessly hugging your hips. You know your Support Team is ready to come forward if you need them as well. You have everything required for the next step of your journey. It's up to you to take it whenever you are ready. Are you ready? Okay. Ready. Set. Here we go!

The Magical Place of *Awareness*

EXPERIENCING THE *Shift*

YOUR *True* SELF
CAVE ONE

You take your next step, your fourth step and find yourself surrounded by a soft, white cloud. You look around, but see nothing, sensing you have entered into a space without any form. It feels like another reality.

As you look ahead, as if in a dream, a red-painted wood gateway appears. Where nothing existed, now it is here, a carved, freestanding structure, the shape of the mathematical sign Pi, with unfamiliar symbols engraved along the high beam. It seems like something abandoned and ancient.

Deep in thought and a bit disoriented, your inner knowing tells you to walk through the doorway, though nothing seems to be on the other side. Hesitant, yet on a deep level trusting the feeling, you make the decision to continue on. At that exact same moment, as if propelled by an unknown force, you move through into the cloud.

All at once, you find yourself in an amazing and incredible magical place. It feels real, yet not real. There is a subtle, yet distinct energy, a vibration, you can feel and see everywhere. It is so elusive, but almost tangible. Looking around, to your left, you notice a pool of water. It shimmers and sparkles, though there doesn't appear to be any identifiable light source. You turn and walk towards it.

At the outer edge of the pool, a huge boulder blocks any view of what may be beyond. Moving closer, you become mesmerized. To your amazement, the rock seems to not be completely solid. It appears to pulsate. There is a play of light and shadow that creates an unusual effect; the surface changes moment to moment. Time does not exist. You are completely immersed in the experience.

Then, something begins to gently tug at you again. You sense yourself being drawn away from your experience as if coming back from some sort of deep meditation. Feeling compelled to turn around, you do so, and are surprised to see a magnificent forest spreading out as far as the eye can see. Wondering why you hadn't noticed it before, you enter its quiet refuge.

There is something quite magical about this place. Enjoying the scents and sounds of this enchanted forest, you notice a cave up ahead. It beckons to you. As you move towards it, you feel drawn to go inside. You cannot resist. You do not want to resist. As you put one foot in front of the other, you are curious as to what you will find.

As you enter the cave, you are stunned by the radiant beauty that greets you. The walls are all made of quartz crystals of different colors and shapes. There is a faint scent of roses. As your eyes adjust, you notice something at the very end of the cave. You walk towards it. There in the far corner, somehow out of place, yet perfect just as it is, stands an old fashioned gilded full- length floor mirror. Nothing else is in this interior space.

Once in front of the mirror, you look into it and reflected back is an image. You know that it is YOU. Yet, it is different. As you look more closely, you realize that you are glowing. Your beauty is radiating out. Swirling colors of emerald green, ruby red, violet, purple, and gold are coming from you, and you are encircled in deep rose and white light. A rainbow of beautiful colors is above your head. You cannot take your eyes off of your reflection in the mirror.

From somewhere deep within, you hear a voice say, "You are beautiful. You are a gift.

You are unique. You are a jewel." And you know this to be the Truth. Time does not exist. Only the experience is real. You feel invigorated and alive, yet a bit pleasantly overwhelmed. After what feels like hours, you look around for a place to sit. Noticing a natural crevice in the crystal wall of the cave, you decide to sit down for awhile. To your delight it is surprisingly comfortable. Free of all thoughts. Experiencing the beauty within. You allow yourself to simply be.

The cave is quiet. Time passes. No one is around. Somehow you know that what you are experiencing is transformational. You are aware you are learning something about yourself which is profound, at this very moment. You know you are awake, yet feel like you are in a dream. You realize you are changing, something is shifting inside. You can sense it with your entire being.

After awhile, you decide to open up your Experiencing the *SHIFT* roadmap. You wonder what the pages will contain. You feel a burning and deep need to understand what is taking place. You are wondering, "What does this experience mean? What is happening to me?"

You open the book. The words seem to come to life, to fill the cave. You read, "In this moment, right now, you are experiencing your TRUE SELF." Each word resonates with TRUTH, each word vibrates through your entire being. You feel your inner strength grow.

"Your True Self is who you truly are. It is your Soul. It is your Essence. It is YOU. Your True Self is kind, compassionate and wise. Your True Self is the source of your creativity and your inner power. Because you are connected to your True Self, you feel good and have a wonderful sense of well-being. You are connected to your power source, to your strength, to your Center. You are connected to that which allows you to create a wonderful life. It is the source that will provide fuel for your upcoming life's journey."

You realize that what you had just seen and experienced at the mirror was your True Self. You are amazed and in awe. You had no idea. You love this feeling and don't want to ever lose it. You want with every part of your being to always see yourself as you did when you looked into the mirror. You realize that in order to keep this feeling you must always be in touch with your True Self. But how do you do it without the mirror or once you have left the cave?

Hoping to find the answer to your questions in the roadmap, you continue to read further.

There on the page is just what you were looking for, the instructions on how to feel this amazing feeling again. "A Moment in Time" is the title. "Now close your eyes and relax. Take a few deep breaths and let your mind wander back in time. Search your memories for a moment in time when you felt the same feeling you just had in front of the mirror."

You search until your find an experience when you felt alive and at peace, on your own, when you felt you could do anything and all was good in your world. You read on, "Now, close your eyes and relax."

Having found your memory, you immerse yourself in it. You allow yourself to re-experience the emotions and the sense of well-being that you had at the original time of the experience. You stay with your inner experience. Time evaporates.

Then, you open your eyes. You cannot help notice that the emotions and the experience you just had are still with you in the here and now. As incredible as it seems, you are feeling the same way as you did when you looked in the mirror and experienced your True Self.

You feel so great, so alive! You know that you can now close your eyes at anytime and become connected to your True Self and this wonderful feeling. Looking down on your lap is the roadmap, and it says, "You have just tapped into your inner source of power. The source of power to create what you most desire comes from within yourself. It comes from knowing who you truly are and being connected to yourself, to your True Self, to your Center."

"You have, and always have had, the ability to go after your dreams. You have all that you need. Your ability to tap into this strength and power is related to the degree of your connectivity to the source of this power, your True Self. The more you are able to connect to your inner and True Self, the more you will be able to create the happiness you want. This ability is absolutely essential and is the most important one in transforming your life."

It also dawns on you that you are feeling really good about yourself, too. You wonder if somehow this feeling is related to the new experience of being connected to your True Self. You go to your roadmap to find out. It says that your True Self is kind, compassionate and understanding. Your True Self does not judge. It is not critical of yourselves or of others. When you are connected to your True Self, you are accepting and understanding of human frailties. You feel good about who you are. Your True Self is confident and knows that you are perfect in your imperfection.

You continue reading, "The True Self is called by some, the Soul. The Soul comes into our human form to actualize itself. To do so, it must learn from life experiences. Inherent to the learning process is making mistakes." You recall William Shakespeare's words, "To err is human."

You read on, "Your Soul, your True Self is perfect just as it is. To be human is to make mistakes. Thus, you are just as you are meant to be, perfect in your imperfection. Self-acceptance, free from judgment, loving yourself, comes from the True Self. Your True Self, your Soul, has a purpose. Its purpose is to learn, grow and utilize the opportunity life presents in order to actualize your True Self in the world."

"Self-acceptance together with the openness and willingness to grow and evolve leads to greater happiness and fulfillment. The True Self contains much wisdom and understanding. When we are connected to it, we are in a state of peace and harmony."

You are stunned. You realize that what you had always felt in your heart, who you always believed yourself to be, is actually real. You want to write down all of your thoughts, feelings and the new realizations you are having, so that you don't forget them.

You take out your Experiencing the SHIFT Journal and beautiful pen from your toolbelt and begin writing. You also write down the experience you had when you had closed your eyes and connected to your True Self. You are curious to see if there were other times in your life when you had an intense experience of your True Self.

You are excited to add more about your other experiences in your journal. But for now, you decide to close your journal. Right now, you simply want to immerse yourself in the joy and peace coming from within. You go to put your journal, gold pen and your roadmap, Experiencing the *SHIFT*, back into your toolbelt when the book slips out of your hand and opens to a page. You look to see what is written.

It says that some people discovered, when closing their eyes, that they were unable to connect with a past experience, unable to remember a time when they felt the emotions described above, afraid of never having had the experience of connecting with their True Self.

You read on, "If you have difficulty right now connecting with a past experience, do not be concerned. In time, these profound and rich moments of feeling connected will be remembered. Know that every person has had these moments of connection in his or her lifetime. Each and every person has a True Self."

You close your eyes, wanting to reflect on these written words and begin to doze off. In what feels like a dream, a woman emerges. You recognize her. She is the same person who had approached you on your Third Step, offering to be part of your Support Team. Now, here she is, together with the other members as well. You cannot quite make them out, but you can certainly hear them. They all seem to be chiming in to share something with you.

You begin to decipher what they are saying. "I experienced my True Self as a child, holding my mother's hand as we crossed the street. It felt SO big and I felt so safe." Another member shares his experience of feeling elated after an interview. One after another, members of your support team share their moments in time.

One after another chime in, "I felt my True Self when dancing to music at home alone",

"As a kid at my championship game, it was the most amazing feeling when my baseball bat made contact with the ball and I knew that I had hit my first home run!"

One after another chimes in, sharing their moments in time while swimming laps in the pool, taking a walk along the beach, or just sitting and looking at their children playing in the yard. There was a pause and unexpectedly another member shared, "I felt my soul soar when I went back to a moment in time when I performed the Rhapsody in Blue by George Gershwin and felt the passion of the music in the depth of my heart and entire being."

There is a moment of silence and then the woman smiles and says, "All the members of the team are so excited to be here with you as you take these initial steps on your new path. They hope that by sharing their experiences, it will help bring forth your own memories of when you had moments of deep connection to your True Self."

As you hear her last words, you feel grateful that you were able to tap into a past experience and are excited to do so again soon. You also realize that how many other people have the desire and have made the decision to experience greater happiness and peace in their lives. You wonder if this insight will change the way you perceive people as you move forward on your new path.

Before having a chance to think about this any further, you hear a noise. You know there is nothing to fear. You feel yourself, in this dream state, turning your head in the direction it is coming from and are surprised to see that someone else has entered the cave and is walking towards you. It is a guy, about 5'9", with short dirty-blond hair. You think he looks like he is in his mid-twenties and wonder why he is here. He appears upbeat and seems to know you. He doesn't look familiar.

As he gets closer, he calls out your name. Reaching out his hand, he takes your hand in his in a warm handshake. He proceed to introduce himself as another one of the members of your Support Team. "Wow", you think. "This is pretty sweet."

As you listen, he begins to speak. "I, too, am traveling on my own personal new path and have my own Support Team helping me all the time. I offered to be a part of your Team so I could provide the same type of support to you that has been so very valuable to me! When I first experienced my True Self in the mirror and then closed my eyes, it felt so good, I didn't want it to end. I was quite startled when the next emotion I felt was fear!"

"I remember thinking, 'Something is going to happen to take this feeling away.' One of the members of my Support Team is this great therapist and he helped me realize that this fear had been created from past experiences. As a child and teenager, whenever I had been connected to my True Self, feeling confident and excited about my abilities and the future, something would happen that would shatter my dream. It was taken away. Nothing good ever seemed to last for too long during those years."

"The emotion of fear is one I had lived with for a very long time. On my new path, I have been able to find the source of the fear, heal from it and then release it. I now am able to feel excited without fear shutting it down and am able to feel my True Self more often now."

"I am so happy you have been able to tap into the strength which comes from your True Self and have found the courage to move forward on your new path. I will be here to provide any additional support you may need if fear should arise. I have helped others to allow themselves to experience the emotion, to recognize it for what it is, and to choose to go after what they truly want."

He then turns to leave and walks out the way he first came in. Just before exiting the cave, he looks back around and waves his hand, saying, "Know that I am here if you need me. I will feel your heart and I'll come to you."

You are a bit stunned, but are grateful to have him as a part of your Support Team. You begin to wonder if any fear will arise from within at a later date. Though you hadn't felt any trepidation during this early part of your journey, you know that at some point, you very well may. You are relieved you will be able to turn to your new Team Member if you find that you are in need of his support.

Your vision begins to clear as if awakening from a dream. You look around, realizing you are still in the unbelievably awe-inspiring cave, alone! All of sudden, you feel a bit disoriented. You start to wonder if all this is just a dream or if it is actually real? How could this be? You know what you are experiencing. It is SO real. But how could it be?

Your head is filled with so much new information and ideas. Thoughts are swirling around and around. You are cognizant that you have already had a some truly profound experiences here in this special space. You know that contained within them is a real opportunity to learn and grow. You want to reflect on these incredible experiences and their lessons, but feel a bit overwhelmed. You decide, though with some sadness, to leave this wonderful place and get a bit of fresh air.

YOUR *False* SELF
CAVE TWO

As you put the roadmap, Experiencing the *SHIFT*, back into your toolbelt, you find yourself thinking," Boy, awareness of my True Self is pretty intense and so is the knowledge that I am not alone. This journey is already quite an adventure!" As you walk across and then out of the cave, your mind is clear of all thought. It feels like some sort of alternate state.

You are back in the magical forest, enjoying wandering aimlessly, allowing yourself to be completely immersed in this wondrous moment. Time passes. How much time, you are not sure. Not quite knowing how, you find yourself again at the edge of the pool of water you had noticed when you first entered this mystical reality.

You move closer, peering into its still waters. They sparkle, light dancing on the surface, seeming to reflect what you are feeling inside, alive and yet calm, excited and somehow still. A wonderful state of relaxation moves throughout your entire body, and a perfect place to lie down next to the calm pool of water beckons. Sinking gently into the soft rich earth, a deep, peaceful sleep washes over you. Time passes. How much time you are not certain.

Feeling rested and renewed, your eyes open. As your vision clears, you are a bit perplexed by what you notice at the opposite edge of the pond. You cannot put your finger on it. It is the familiar rock boulder but there is something different about it now. What is it about the rock that seems to have changed?

As much as you want to take a closer look, you are also so curious and cannot wait to look around and discover what other incredible mysteries are contained within this magical world. You feel ready to move on to see what awaits you. Tapped into your inner strength and courage, you are ready to go deeper into the forest, the Magical Place of Awareness.

You stand up, stretch, and begin to walk. You walk deeper into the forest, in a new direction. After some time, you notice another cave. Having had such an amazing experience in the first cave, you do not hesitate to go towards this second cave even though a fog seems to have moved in. You enter without hesitation. Immediately, you feel ill at ease.

Though you cannot see anything, you can feel something repulsive. As your eyes adjust, you can see that this second cave is just like the first in shape and size but instead of walls made of quartz crystal, this one is made of volcanic rock. Everything is dark. The colors of the wall are black, gray, brown and a dark, eerie red. There is a slight stench. You are about to turn around and leave, when you see at the very end of the cave a shiny mirror, just like the one in the quartz crystal cave.

As much as you are repulsed, you are drawn to the mirror. The thought of experiencing your True Self and seeing it reflected in the mirror is stronger than any of the ugliness around you. You run to the mirror and look into it, expecting to see what you had seen before.

To your horror, the image reflected back to you is so repulsive that you feel sick to your stomach. You know it is YOU. You can see that it is your inner ugliness pouring out. Instead of beautiful and pure white light, there are dark dull colors like those on the inner wall of the cave. Instead of a rainbow above your head, all that exists are blobs of gray. You recognize what is in front of you and avert your eyes from the mirror as quickly as possible.

From somewhere deep within, you hear a voice say,"You are stupid. You are a mess-up. You have no will power. You are an addict. You are worthless. You are ugly. You will never be loved." Time no longer exists. You do not exist. You are weak. You feel your power completely drain out of your body.

You know you have to leave but you cannot move. The air is toxic. You can barely breathe. You force yourself to put one foot in front of the other. You have to get out. As you make your way to the other end of the cave, you hear something. It is as if it is coming from far away.

As you try to listen, this is what you hear. "The image reflected back to you from the mirror is your False Self. It is not you. Your False Self is not who you truly are. It is who you may believe you are. Your False Self was created by other people's negative judgments and criticisms. It was created by how others may have perceived you or made you feel about yourself. It was formed by other people's words and actions."

"If you see yourself as bad, weak, a failure, unlovable or unworthy, this is your False Self that you believe to be who you really are. It is not who you are. It was created the moment you first began to believe the negative, critical words that others said to you. It was at this moment that you started to disconnect from your True Self."

"The confusion as to who you truly are originated as you began to doubt yourself at a young age. You stated to doubt your own perception of yourself. With the passing years, you had many different experiences with opportunities to grow and learn, making occasional mistakes along the way, as all human being do. Instead of receiving love, understanding and guidance, you were criticized and judged. Your False Self grew as did your confusion. In time, you began to ask,"Who am I?""

"Oh, my gosh", the words come pouring out from deep within. You realize that what you had just seen and experienced at the mirror is not who you really are. It was your False Self. You know it exists within you but it is not you. It is dark and toxic just like the cave you are in.

As you allow this realization to permeate your being, you can feel some of your energy return. You smile as you realize it is coming from your True Self. You cannot wait to get out of this horrible place. You wonder how you ever believed that the image staring back at your from the mirror could be YOU. Feeling like you are moving in slow motion, you proceed towards the entrance to the cave all the while asking yourself, "When did I first begin to believe that the False Self was who I am?"

As if downloaded into your mind, this is what you receive."When you were an infant and a very young child, you knew your True Self. You were joyous and happy and the world looked bright. You were connected to your True Self. You felt connected to everything and everyone around you. You felt safe. You felt secure. You felt loved, cared for and protected. You looked into your parents' eyes and saw your own beauty reflected back to you. All was good."

"Then, as time went on, something inside began to hurt. You didn't like the feeling. You knew something was wrong. There were moments when you felt less secure, when you would look into your parents' faces and did not like what you saw reflected back. You began to doubt your own beauty. You began to not feel as loved, cared for and protected. You didn't' understand what was going on. You felt less joy. You didn't feel happy inside. You wondered if there was something wrong with you."

"This was the moment that you first began to disconnect from your True Self. This was the moment that you allowed others to determine your own worth. This is when you first began to give away your power, the power inherent in your True Self. This was the moment that you learned about judgment, criticism and that love can be withdrawal. This is when you first lost you sense of security. This is when your False Self began to take form."

With this realization, you step over the threshold of the cave. You are out. You are free. You don't remember how you got from one end of the cave to the other but it doesn't matter because you have survived. You feel better. Now you understand what you had experienced from the moment you entered the cave until this very moment.

Grateful to feel connected once again to your True Self, you know with every fiber of your being that you will NEVER again let yourself believe that your False Self is who you truly are. You realize that the False Self is an illusion, one you had believed to be real for a very, very long time.

Now you understand the pain always felt

deep inside. It was coming from believing your False Self was who you truly were. You now know when and how your False Self originated. With this new awareness, some of your innate power returns. You feel lighter. You have been in the dark cave and are more determined than ever to really begin living.

You know this experience has provided you with a new understanding. You know you are growing and changing through the new knowledge and greater awareness gained. You feel your power returning and are feeling more centered. You are connecting again to your true source of strength, your True Self. You are beginning to Experience the *SHIFT*.

THE Copper SCALE

You are blown away. Through your experiences in the two caves, a clearer vision of who you truly are has begun to emerge. For some reason, you feel like the fog inside is beginning to lift. Absorbing the majestic and peaceful surroundings, you feel the forest beckon you into its arms. You move deeper into its cool and comforting refuge. Walking amongst the trees, you are lulled by the beautiful music of the wind as it moves through the leaves of the magnificent old trees. It feels so soothing to be out in nature. It feels so good to breath in the fresh air.

You look up at the sky and see birds of all different shapes and colors. Without realizing it, unconsciously you begin to follow them as they fly and soar through the air. You are mesmerized. After some time has passed, you realize your walk had taken you deep into the forest. It is so beautiful and enchanting here.

You decide to walk a bit further, but before you get too far, something suddenly takes you out of your reverie. You cannot believe your eyes. There, in the clearing up ahead, is the most unusual and unexpected object. You stop in your tracks. Right in front of you is a HUGE Scale!! It resembles an old-fashioned measuring scale. It has a large copper bowl at each end and stretches up to the sky, rising above the ancient treetops. As you watch, it appears to be moving very slowly, up and down, a bit like a teeter-totter.

Flying above and around the scale are birds, lots and lots of them, each of a different color. Some are orange, some red. Others are purple. Some have polka dots of yellow and pink and others have stripes of tan and green. Some are black and others are brown. They are all flying to and fro, coming and going, dropping something into the bowls and leaving with their beaks empty.

You find yourself curious and amused. You wonder what is going on. You are immensely curious regarding what the birds are doing. What it is that they are placing into the bowls, and why is the scale continuously going up and down?

You draw closer with hopes to find out. To your utter surprise, you see letters. As you peer more closely, you realize the birds are carrying words back and forth. You notice the black and brown birds are dropping the words into the copper bowl on your left and some of the brightly colored birds are dropping their own words into the other bowl. Each time they do, words from the bowl on the left simply evaporate. You observe the scale tipping to the side with the most words. As the scale goes up and down, you peer more intently wanting to make out the specific words being placed in each bowl.

Astonishingly, some of the words dropped into the left bowl by the dark feathered birds are, "lazy, fat, stupid, failure, weak." As they drop in these ugly, mean and cruel words, a wave of sadness encompasses you. As more and more words are dropped into the same bowl, you observe the beautiful words evaporate. Feeling a knot in your stomach, nausea, pain and a strange urge begin to overtake you.

You notice you are feeling the same way you did when you were seeing your False Self in the mirror of the second cave. You realize this is the same feeling you have been carrying within most of your life. You gaze over to the other bowl on your right and watch the bright colored birds dropping in the, more words, "intelligent, wonderful, strong, beautiful, successful." As more of these words are placed into this bowl on the scale, you feel a sense of relief, the pain begins to subside. You begin to feel better.

The beautifully colored birds continue to make their delivery. As the scale continues to tip, you feel lighter and lighter. Just like a seesaw, the scale continue to go up and down. The magical scale seems to *SHIFT* according to the words it weighs. As more words are dropped into one copper bowl, the negative and hurtful words simply disappear from the other. Released, too, are the negative, toxic emotions you had been experiencing. Wow! How interesting is this! Somehow you know that the work of the birds is sacred.

As you watch, there are more and more colorful birds flying around, placing their words into their copper bowl, you realize that the bowl on the left side, empty of words, has reached the forest floor. The bowl on the right is soaring above the trees as though the positivity of the words has lifted it into the air. A feeling of peace and joy begin to envelop you. You feel like you did when you were in the first cave connecting with your True Self. You stop and take in a deep, wonderful breath. The wind gently blows and a feeling of joy and peace surround you.

You cannot contain yourself any longer. You know that you will be able to understand what you are observing and experiencing once you open up your Experiencing the *SHIFT* roadmap. Looking for a place to sit, you notice a beautiful Laurel Tree. You stroll over and allow yourself to relax, sinking down into the dried fallen leaves, resting your back against the big, sturdy, welcoming trunk.

Comfortable and now settled in, you open up your roadmap and begin to read from where you left off. "Within your being, you each have your own internal scale. One bowl contains all the kind and compassionate words you tell yourself about who you are and the other bowl holds all of the critical and judgmental words you say to yourself throughout the day."

"The wise and supportive words come from your True Self which has its own voice, the True Voice. The critical, judgmental words come from your False Self and has its own voice, the False Voice. The False Voice was created as you internalized the judgmental and critical statements made by one or both of your parents and other significant people in your childhood. It became louder as others in your life used the same or similar words."

"As time went on, you began to speak to yourself in the same way. The more often you were harsh with yourself, the louder the False Voice became. Within, you have a scale like the one in the forest. The balance of your inner scale depends on the words that you let yourself absorb and believe and the words that you say to yourself."

Without thinking about it, you close the book and place it into your toolbelt. You are stunned. As you look at the huge scale in the forest, you feel another *SHIFT* occur. You ask yourself, "How could all of this been going on within myself and I didn't even know it?"

From some unknown source, you hear, "When you were born, the scale didn't exist. All that existed was one bowl, a beautiful shiny one. At the beginning, the brightly colored birds were all around you, bringing words of love and safety, and placing them in your bowl."

"Then, the darkly colored birds began to enter into your world. They needed somewhere to place their hateful and hurtful words. A new bowl and with it the scale was created." As you look closely at your inner scale, you can see, to your dismay, that the bowl filled with critical words is almost overflowing while the other bowl with the kind, loving words is difficult to see.

You feel a determination well up from the very depth of your being. It is the same feeling that you had when you moved onto your third step. You know, more than ever, that you will do whatever it takes to feel good. You want to be free of the False Voice and the pain that follows. You don't know how it will happen, but you have more faith and trust that this new path that you are on will take you there.

In deep thought, contemplating and processing all of this new information, you begin to think about the type of comments others have made to you and those you have said to yourself. You think of different situations and challenges you have faced, reflecting on whether you had judged yourself harshly or had been compassionate towards yourself.

As you lean against the Laurel Tree, you can feel the sturdiness of it's mighty trunk against your back. It feels so strong and provides you with a much needed sense of being grounded. As you lean your back against the trunk something pushes against your thigh. Realizing that it is your Experiencing the Shift Journal, you take out it and open to a fresh page.

Using the beautiful pen, you draw a scale. The scale has two bowls, just like the scale that you just observed earlier deep within the magical forest. In your journal, next to the scale on the right, you begin to write down the kind, supportive words that you hear coming from your True Voice. You then write down, next to the scale on the left, all of the critical, judgmental, hurtful ones that comes from your False voice.

With amazement, you discover how many more words are on the left side of the page than on the right. You realize just how strong and loud your False Voice really is and how soft your True Voice has become. You realize how few words are in one bowl and how many are in the other. You close the journal, feeling tired and a bit worn out.

The *Laurel* Tree

Shutting your eyes, desiring to be free of thought for awhile, you find yourself falling into a deep sleep. After some time has passed, you become aware that you are in the middle of a dream. You find yourself in an empty movie theater. You wonder where everyone else is and than realize that it is actually a private showing just for you! The movie starts. You feel like you are watching an old-fashioned home movie in the comfort of your own private theater, aware that the scenes unfolding in front of you are from your own life.

As you gaze at the screen, you watch as one scene after another reveals specific experiences from you childhood and youth. You watch one scene after another. As you watch one you cannot stop laughing and in another you cannot stop crying. You observe as each scene unfolds.

Contained within the movie are not only the external events, but the internal ones you experienced as well. As the movie of your life continues, many different emotions arise. Time goes on and then the movie comes to an end. The reel of film is empty. The lights in the movie theater turn on. At that moment, you awaken.

Expecting to wake up in your home, you slowly become aware that you are still here in the Magical Place of Awareness. You feel like you are in a dream. You just had a dream, yet you know that you are awake. Your sense of reality is a bit fuzzy." This is becoming quite a common occurrence," you think. You recognize you no longer feel quite the same you did when you first started out on your new path.

Trying to make sense of everything, you think back to the dream you just had where you were in the movie theater. It felt so real. It was as if you had been taken back in time, re-experiencing the past. Feeling compelled to write down the thoughts and emotions you had just experienced, you open your journal.

Turning to a new fresh page, you inscribe on the top a name you choose to represent one of the scenes in your movie. Next, you draw a vertical line down the middle of the page.

On one side, you write down the thoughts you had while in the first scene and on the other side, you write down the emotions. As one page is completed, you turn to the next and continue this process for each scene, each event, from your life.

As you go from one scene to another, it dawns on you how much each one had contributed to your own self-image. You can see how your False Self was created and took hold, and when the connection with your True Self started to become stronger. You are now even more keenly aware of the words that were spoken by others in the past and how they made you feel.

You realize that your thoughts about yourself and your actions and behaviors that followed differed in each scene. You now also recognize how some of the beliefs that you presently have about people and life were formed. You are intrigued about the formation process of the beliefs you have today. Some of these beliefs are about yourself. Some are about addiction. Some of these beliefs are about the meaning of life. And other are about the goodness of people.

You decide to write all your thoughts and beliefs down. You want to understand yourself on a new and deeper level. Enjoying feeling the tree trunk along your back and the peacefulness of the forest, time passes as you write in your special journal.

This magical place, with all of its dream-like qualities seems more authentic than the concrete reality of what occurred in the past. You are deep in thought when someone seemingly out of nowhere appears. It is a woman in a flowing gown. You close your journal and place it in your toolbelt quietly.

She greets you with a smile and the two of you begin to talk. She asks what brought you to the forest. Sensing that you can trust her and feeling a need to share, you begin to talk to her about the new path that you are on and what you have learned. She is empathetic and shares that she too has been traveling on her own new path for quite awhile.

You begin to think that she might be another member of your Support Team. Almost as if reading your mind, she introduces herself as one and asks if you have experienced the "movie theater." You answer in the affirmative. Feeling emboldened, you ask her if she feels comfortable confiding in you what she had seen while watching her "movie." She opens up as she sits down on the cool leaf-covered ground.

"One of the scenes that unfolded, had originally taken place, when I was a little girl. I actually watched a number of scenes that were all very similar. Most of my life, I spent a lot of time at home with my mother. I was an only child and my father worked a lot and went out of town for business often."

"In one scene, I saw myself at age six in the living room of our house, asking my mother if I could have a playdate with a few friends after school. My mother looked at me and told me that I could not. I had never had a friend over before nor had I gone out to play without my mother watching me."

"I remember feeling that somehow I was betraying her by asking. She told me that it is better not to get together with friends, except in school. She made me feel that it would be unsafe. I felt sad, guilty and lonely. The belief I was not good enough and had to deny my needs to be loved, took shape. I never did have a friend come over or have a play date throughout the time I lived at home."

You feel bad for your Support Team member. You express your feeling to her and can sense that she appreciates your kindness and empathy. She then says, "We all have thoughts and create beliefs based on our own personal experiences. From this experience and other similar ones growing up, I came to believe that I was responsible for my mother's feelings, that the world was an unsafe place and I was only safe when I was with my mother. I came to believe that I was not a good person because a good person would not cause pain to a loved one."

"I was dependent, lonely, sad and shy. I carried this pain with me throughout my childhood and into my adulthood. I wanted love. I needed love. I did whatever I could to receive it. Sometimes, I would find relief from the pain when engaging in different activities. As a child, it was with food, especially sweets. As I got older, it was with alcohol and then later with drugs. Each allowed me to escape, but only for awhile."

"As I grew up and became an adult, I continued to go through life in this way. I lost some weight and started having sex with almost anyone, but only after drinking a lot of alcohol or getting high, longing to feel a connection. I had developed a certain way of being in the world, hoping it would give me the best chance of escaping the loneliness and finding love. When I stepped onto my new path, I was still searching."

She went on. "Here, in the Magical Place of Awareness, I discovered when and how my False self was formed. My False Self believed that I was dependent on others to feel good, to feel safe. My False Self believed I was not worthy of having what I wanted. My False Self believed that no matter what I did, I was still unlovable. As a little girl, I simply wanted to go out and play with the other kids in my neighborhood and with friends from school. Was that too much to ask? Now I know that it was healthy. It was mother who was not."

"With each step on my new path, I met people who were on their own journey. Some of them also had used something or someone to numb their pain. Some used food, alcohol, drugs and sex, like I did. Others shared how gambling, smoking cigarettes, cutting, and obsessively playing video games gave them the same relief, though always temporary. I also, met people who told me how they would exercise or work excessively to avoid their own painful feelings and unwanted thoughts."

"I came to realize, while talking and spending time with my Team Members, that when given the love and support we need while growing up, positive thoughts and beliefs about ourselves and the world are created. When we do not received what we need, the belief there is something inherently wrong with us begins to form."

"It is at that moment in time, we start to question our own worth and to believe the critical, judgmental words expressed to us by others could possibly be true. Our False Self is created. We begin to disconnect from our True Self."

"We start to internalize these False thoughts and ideas about ourselves and about how the world works. We begin to adsorb and accept other people's negative and incorrect views as our own. We internalize the critical, harsh words of others. Our False Self and False Voice come into existence. Time passes."

"Each experience we have and the messages and beliefs that we internalize add to our sense of Self. This process occurs within every person. For you, depending on your experiences over time, you may have come to believe that you are not deserving of all the wonderful things that life has to offer."

"When this was happening within me, I didn't realize at the time that I had the power to feel good about myself. I believed that the power to feel good was dependent on others. Engaging in behaviors temporarily numbed the pain only to create more pain, more confusion, more difficulties. They allowed me to disconnect from the pain. By doing so, though, I was disconnecting from my True Self."

"Here on the new path, I came to realize that I could be happy and that this wonderful feeling came from being connected to my True Self, the source of my joy and peace. Having identified the behaviors that led to some of the loss of this connection, I used the Gifts that you too will receive here, to stay connected. I reaffirmed my decision to do whatever it takes to be happy. In my case, it was no longer drinking, using and having sex based on physical attraction to someone who didn't really care about me."

"I now know that I am a good person. I feel safe and secure, free of guilt, shame and fear. My new thoughts and feelings created a *SHIFT*. I could feel the scale moving within. I started to feel better about myself and about life."

"As I moved further along on my path, I realized that what my False Voice, the critical, judgmental voice I heard in my head, was telling me was not true. As I was able to hear my True Voice, I felt better. With each step on my new path, I have gained a tremendous amount of understanding about myself and others and the world. With each step, I took actions that supported my happiness and well-being. I now have a clearer view of who I really am and feel more connected to my

True Self than I ever had before. I now have lots of real friends too!"

You wonder how she achieved this connection and how she discovered her True Self. You find yourself asking her how she did this, how she was able to feel so much better. She smiles as she stands up and reaches out her hand, taking your hand in hers. You stand up, too, and follow her, letting her lead you, unaware of your destination, yet trusting her completely."

As you walk through the forest, she continues to share, "Know that you carry within yourself, as I do, false beliefs. These beliefs are THOUGHTS attached to very powerful emotions. With each step on your new path, your True Voice will become louder and your False Voice will automatically begin to lose some of its power."

"As this occurs, you will start to feel better. You will start to have hope that maybe you can find what you are looking for. In time, you will discover your innate ability to create more of what you truly desire. Now that you have a new understanding of the truth of what is taking place within you, hope will follow."

"Going forward on your path, you, will learn how to make your True Voice louder and how to connect and stay connected with who you truly are, your True Self. With each step, you will come to know that it is your birthright to be at peace. This is what happened to me."

"It's great that you have already started to identify and write down in your journal the various beliefs, thoughts and values that you hold. As you continue to do so, important insights and understanding regarding how they were created and when and why you have incorporated them into your life will be gained."

As you reflect on her words and on what you had learned from watching the movie of your life, re-experiencing past experiences and noticing how some of the beliefs about yourself were created, you suddenly feel an overwhelming feeling of sadness and pain.

You look up at the sky above and notice some of the black birds you had seen dropping words onto the Copper Scale and begin to feel a terrible and powerful urge. You begin thinking about times when you had felt this uncomfortable sensation before. The feeling is strange, yet familiar. You remember how very much you had wanted to get away from this urge and unsettling sensation.

Feeling slightly in a daze, you return your gaze to your Support Team member. She begins to speak, though her voice seems far, far away. "Take my hand and I will take you to a place where you will gain a greater understanding of yourself and the life you have led before entering this Magical Place of Awareness. It will take much courage. I'll be right here with you. The choice is yours."

The pain you have been feeling intensifies. Thoughts begin to swirl in your head. You want so much to escape from this internal suffering and to numb it up as you have done in the past. You want to be free. Free from the pain, free from the suffering, free from the anxiety, free from the anger, sadness, guilt and shame, even if it will be temporary.

Your mind goes back, for some reason, to the moment when you were looking at your True Self in the mirror just a short time ago. A feeling begins to grow within. It is the same feeling you had back then. You know how much you want to feel the feeling again.

You decide, just as you did when you took the second step onto your new path, that you will do whatever it takes to be happy. To be free from your False Voice telling you how terrible you are. To be free from the pain that seems to be a constant unwanted guest.

You turn to your support team member, and nod that you are ready to go. You decide, just as you did when you took the second step onto your new path, that you will do whatever it take to feel joy and peace and to be permanently and completely free of this uncomfortable urge—the urge to numb the pain. You know, too, that you are willing and ready to face what is up ahead. You both stand up together and as your Team Member looks deeply into your eyes she says, "OK Let me show you something."

She takes your hand and asks you to close your eyes. For some reason, you trust her. You close your eyes and can feel a powerful energy force surrounding the two you. You feel as if you are in the middle of a storm, energy swirling all around and around, yet in the center it is calm. You allow the energy to envelop you. Time stands still. Suddenly everything becomes quiet. Curious, you open your eyes and are horrified at the scene before you.

You are in a room with a lot of people who are using and drinking. The music is so loud and the room is filled with smoke. Your Support Team member is there by your side. You realize that you are on the second floor of a huge mansion. She motions for you to follow her, pointing at a balcony at the other end of the room.

As you do so, you look at the people around you. Without trying to, you overhear some of their conversations and think to yourself, "They aren't making any sense." You do not judge. You understand. You have been in rooms like this many, many times. Too many to think about.

As you continue making your way through the smoke-filled entryway, the air becomes heavy. You cannot see your Team Member. It feels like you are moving in slow motion. It is as if you just stepped into one of the scenes in the movie theater while under the Laurel Tree. You can hear a couple in the midst of an argument and realize how judgmental and critical they are being of each other.

At that moment, it is as if a light bulb has gone off in your head. As you listen more closely, you can hear a voice within say, "They are both disconnected from their True Self and are unable to treat each other with love and respect. How can they, if they don't love themselves."

You can see they are high and are not thinking about what they are saying. You know this because it has happened to you over and over. In past relationships you were able to discuss an issue at-hand calmly, but when high everything turned into an argument.

You see now how much alcohol and drugs has interfered with your ability to deal with situations in the past. You want to talk with your Support Team member about these new realizations, but cannot find her up ahead. You turn around looking in every direction.

All of a sudden, you are startled by a loud noise. Looking to see what is going on, you observe that someone just spilled a drink on another person accidentally and the glass broke as it hit the ground. You think to yourself, "That just happened to me not too long ago." Sadness fills you as you think about how you allowed yourself to be in environments just like this one so many times in the past, too many to count, so unhappy, but feeling that there was no where else to go.

The alcohol and drugs helped you survive the pain, numbed your thoughts and emotions, so you could survive until this moment in time when you have made the decision to do whatever it takes to be free to be your True Self in the world, free of addiction.

You peer through the crowd and catch a glimpse of the balcony up ahead and can see your Team Member. You now feel an urgency to reach her. She sees you too and motions for you to join her. As you make your way to her, you notice, across the room, a group of people watching a horse race on the large T.V. screen while cheering for their favorite winner. Everyone seems to be stressed and upset. As you pass a sofa and look at the people eating around the coffee table, they seem robotic as they eat and eat and eat, mindlessly devouring everything in front of them.

Moving closer towards the balcony, you look into a room off to the side filled with bodies, bodies of people having sex, searching for a heart and soul connection with none to be had. Everywhere you look, all the people you see are like shadows. Everyone and everything—void of pleasure, unable to find satisfaction.

Approaching the threshold of the balcony, you cannot wait to step over and cross to the other side. You can feel how much you want to be free. Free from the past. Free from the pain. Free from the loneliness and feelings of emptiness.

A great wave of relief passes over you along with the fresh air, leaving the smoke-filled room and the people within it. You are grateful to finally be free, noticing how different you feel in this moment than how your felt in the past while on the second floor. You are so happy to reconnect with your Team Member. You sense she can see you, who you truly are, and you are able to see her essence, her soul, too. Time and space no longer exist. Only the connection is real.

"Thank you from coming with me. I know this hasn't been easy for you", she says. "My Support Team member brought me here, too, when I first stepped onto my new path. This is the world I lived in for such a long time. When I was a teen, I ran to the second story of this house to get away from the pain below."

"Though deep inside I knew how unhappy I was, I had resigned myself to remaining here in this way. Every once in awhile, I would try to leave this second story, to go downstairs, to the ground floor where I used to live my life, where so many of the people I love lived."

"But whenever I would go down there, using will-power to stay away from alcohol and drugs, there was so much pain. It was as if I didn't have the ability to withstand it for more than what felt like moments. Sometimes it was days, sometimes even a year. But inevitably, the pain became too great and I returned back to this second story, numbing my pain, feeling dead inside."

"Disconnected from my thoughts, disconnected from my feelings, disconnected from my True Self. This went on for many, many years until one day, I discovered there was a way to live on the ground floor and be happy."

As you are listening to this beautiful person in front of you, it was hard to fathom that what she said was true. She seemed so happy and content. You continue to listen and she shares more about her past. "The alcohol and drugs and other unhealthy behaviors helped me survive. By numbing myself, I was able to keep going. Unhappy thoughts just passed by and the painful emotions were muted. At times, I was able to forget about everything and convince myself I was happy and just having fun."

"Everything and everyone that I was attracted to led to more pain. I realized that even the people I was physically attracted to and was looking to connect with on a deeper level, to love and feel loved, were unable to give me what I was looking for because they were empty, too."

"Instead, the feeling of loneliness, confusion, and unworthiness just grew stronger. With all the drama around me, I was distracted and could avoid thinking about what really mattered to me. I could avoid the pain, at least for awhile. I began to believe this was all I deserved and could ever have."

"When I started on my new path, I met individuals who were further along on this path. They let me know they would be honored to be on my Support Team. I gained so much knowledge from them and, as I did so, the confusion I had felt for most of my life began to lift. Those on my Support Team, who had become free from past addictions, shared what they had learned from their Support Team members as well."

You feel something stirring from deep within. You want to know what she had learned. You want to be free of the confusion and pain. "Could you be kind enough to share some of this knowledge with me?" you ask ever so softly. She smiles and motions for us to sit in the comfortable sofa at the end of the balcony and as we sink down into its soft cushions, she begins.

"I remember a time, at 15 years old, that I was getting ready to go to a party. Just before I was about to leave, I got into a terrible argument with my parents. It wasn't the first time. We had been having problems for quite some time. My friend picked me up and as we were driving to the party, I was feeling so angry and hurt. I kept replaying the fight in my head while trying not to have my friend see what was going on, so we could have some fun. When we arrived at our friend's house, I couldn't seem to shake the feeling. I was so upset."

"Someone offered me a drink. Without much thought, I took it and drank it down pretty quickly. All of a sudden, the painful feelings disappeared. So did the thoughts I hadn't been able to get out of my head. At that moment, I discovered a way to feel better and never looked back."

"When I was really intoxicated, I just wanted to enjoy and to forget. Sex and Rock n' Roll became my new way in life. It was really fun at first. I couldn't wait for the weekends to go out and party. Sometimes, I'd go to the casino with my friends and other times to clubs. I felt happy and free until I didn't."

"I started to have hang-overs in the morning and began drinking in the morning to feel 'normal.' My self-worth got even lower after sleeping with someone the night before, having felt at times so close and loved, and at other times feeling invisible, yet always with the same outcome. Never hearing from the person again."

"Over time, I began using the money I made in my part-time job to buy weed and drugs when I couldn't get them from friends for free. I went to the casino thinking I could make some more money, but inevitably whatever I won was lost, plus much, much more."

"I noticed that some of my friends were no longer around. Some had pulled away, not wanting to be around me due the unhealthy people and activities in my life. Others were isolating themselves, shutting out the world and just eating and eating until they were sick."

"When I would see them, they would share about how upset they had been, how much weight they had gained and how awful they felt about themselves, going on and off of diets, gaining and losing weight, some binging and throwing-up. It was so sad to see such beautiful people in so much pain."

"I tried to cut back on drugs and alcohol. I stayed away from people who were engaging in the same behaviors. I was able to do this for awhile and then something would happen. I would feel the pain again and knew what would make it go away."

"I started drinking and using when home alone. This went on for many years until I realized how much these behaviors were impacting the rest of my life. Each relationship I had ended. I knew that part of the reason was due to the unhealthy behaviors I had developed."

"Then something terrible happened and I decided, I really had to stop. I knew I had to. I researched different types of programs and chose the one that sounded the best to me. While participating, it felt great not having anything unhealthy in my body. It was amazing not having arguments with people that I loved."

"I thought I had it. That I was free forever from the pain, free from the addiction. After completing the program, I returned home and felt so good. I felt proud of myself and ready to live my life. And then, slowly it started up all over again. At the beginning, I was able to make choices that supported my happiness, but little by little, all the old behaviors came back again. I was devastated."

"This cycle happened over and over again. I kept trying. It felt so hard. I didn't know if I could do it. Sometimes, I was more successful than other times. My relationships all suffered. I isolated myself from friends and family. My sense of self-esteem was worse than ever. I felt there was no hope, nowhere to go."

"And then, I discovered this new path. As I began to take one step after another, I felt a *SHIFT* taking place, first internally and then in my life. I began to experience what I felt in the True Cave and it was so wonderful. I wanted more. As I moved further along on my new path, I gained the 20 Gifts which allowed me to stay connected to this feeling, regardless of what was going on around me."

"I was able to identify where the urge came from that took control of my actions and thoughts; The urge that I felt unable to resist when I knew with every part of my being that acting on it would lead to great unhappiness within and all around me. In the Healing Oasis, along my new path, I was able to heal the pain from the past, one of the sources of the urge."

"I also chose to be in healthy environments and to be with kind, thoughtful people who supported my new way of being. I discovered what I needed and started to give it to myself and to request the same from others. By giving to myself in this way, the urges became less frequent."

"As I continued to Experience the *SHIFT*, I began to have more and more freedom from the urge that used to take control. Today, I am able to make choices that support my happiness. I rarely feel the urge and if I do, I have the ability to choose my actions."

"My life is so different now. I love the life I have created. I love how I feel about myself.

I make the choice, moment by moment, to continue walking on this path, knowing only too well where a detour would lead me. I am not willing to give up the life I have created to go back to the suffering I was in. The process of *SHIFT* Actualization™ has allowed my Freedom from Addiction. I have become free from its control, free to be me."

You are stunned. "Thank goodness I have been sitting in this comfortable sofa, otherwise I might have fallen over the balcony!" You laugh to yourself. Realizing that you are laughing in the midst of all of this intense information is quite a surprise.

After some time passes, in deep reflection, a question arises in your mind and you ask your Team member, "I, too, have tried many times to change certain behaviors. Sometimes, like you, the change I wanted to create lasted for quite a long time and other times it did not."

"Is there a way that I can continue engaging in these behaviors occasionally and still become free from their control or is it necessary to stop them completely? I really would like to find a way that I can engage in them while still having the control."

You are hoping that your Team Member will suggest a way to continue. You wait in anticipation until she begins. "I know how much pleasure you get initially and how much you want that pleasure in your life. I wanted the same. I asked my Team Member the same question and I'll share with you his response."

He said, "Imagine a line. As long as you have not crossed over the line, you have the ability to choose your actions. You have the ability to decide how much you will engage in a particular activity and are able to follow through on that decision."

"Once the line is crossed, you may choose your actions, but the urge will take over, sometimes sooner, sometimes later. But it always does. Your actions will not be based on your choice, but rather on something else taking control over you."

She continues sharing her own thoughts, "Addiction is very sneaky. It makes you think that you have control because you can act on your decision for awhile, but sooner or later it takes over. If you have crossed the line, you will have control and then you won't."

"My team member shared with me what he had learned on his new path. He found that once a person has crossed the line, in order to become free from addiction, the unhealthy behavior or substance must be removed completely from one's life. I have found the same to be true for myself, too."

This isn't what you want to hear. You know how much you do not want to give up the pleasure you get, until you don't. You share this with your Team Member and she responds. "Many people on the new path spend some time finding out whether they have actually crossed the line. They decide when and where they will make the choice to engage in the behavior."

"With their new level of awareness and understanding, they watch to see if that line has been crossed. If they are able to identify how much they can engage in the behavior without any negative consequences to themselves or others, and have found the balance that works for themselves over a long period of time, then they may have not crossed the line."

"One of my Team Members told me about problems he had been having with his girlfriend before starting on the new path. He shared that the only time they fought was at a social event or afterwards."

"As he began to Experience the *SHIFT*, he became aware arguments occurred only during and after he had been drinking. In his conversations with his girlfriend when sober, she shared feeling disconnected from him at those times because his behavior had changed."

"Here on the new path, he experimented with the amount and type of alcohol he would drink, to see when this behavior change took place. He realized that it would happen after three alcoholic beverages, sometimes after two, depending on the type. He made the decision to have no more than the two drinks whenever he went out, and found that he was able to do so over the course of many years."

"He shared with me that he believes he hadn't crossed the line and reports that all is well in the home front. He also was excited to tell me about how much more heartfelt intimacy he was now experiencing in his relationship after making this change and having receiving the 20 Gifts along his new path."

"I've discovered that most people here on the path, who are asking themselves this question, find that usually sooner than later, the behavior takes control and that they have crossed the line. With this new information, if they want to Experience the *SHIFT* and have Freedom from Addiction, they have chosen to eliminate the substance and behavior from their life using the Gifts and Manifesting Charms they gain along their new path."

"As you continue moving forward, you will find the answer to your question. You will discover when the urge arises, if it is when you have emotional pain or when you are around certain people, places and things."

"You will discover in your journey what it is that you need and how to give it to yourself. This process can allow you to have the freedom you desire with all of your being. Here, on your new path, you will begin to make new choices that support your happiness and a life filled with peace."

You can feel the scale within you begin to shift. You know how very much you want to be truly happy and at peace. You begin wondering if you have crossed the line and from deep within, looking honestly at yourself, you know you have.

You have a sinking feeling in your stomach and begin to feel sick with fear. "What if I decide to no longer engage in the behavior and then it happens again." You blurt out in pain, "What if this happens when I am on my new path. Then this won't work either."

With deep compassion, she shares. "Most people who are on their new path will hit pebbles, where they engage in the old behavior, along the way. If they don't see them beforehand, they may end up taking a detour off of the path. Some get back onto the path. Others never do."

"As you gain new Gifts and Charms, a greater awareness and understand of yourself and others, you will enable you to stop and notice the pebble before tripping over it and then going on the detour. Instead, you are able to look at the pebble, learn what it is made up of and gain new knowledge and life skills, and continue on your path."

"Having learned from the past, some pebbles will never come up again, or if they do, they will be smaller, and when you see them ahead, you will be able to walk around them instead of stumbling. Over time, there will be fewer and fewer pebbles, and you will have gained much wisdom, awareness and knowledge on your journey."

She adds almost as an afterthought, "By the way, here on the new path, we don't use the word 'addiction.' Instead, we call it for what it is, something that has the ability to take control of our thoughts and actions." You like the way that makes you feel. You can see how much words affect how you feel.

At that moment, you hear laughter. It is coming from the ground floor below. You stand up and look over the balcony. A wave of emotions flows through your entire body. You can feel how very much you want to live your life free from pain, free from urges and thoughts of drinking and using. Free from unhealthy relationships and from hurting yourself.

You close your eyes, remembering how you felt in the cave when you experienced your True Self. You are somewhat aware of your support team member taking your hand in hers. Time passes. How much, you do not know.

You feel a light breeze across your face and through your hair. You open your eyes and to your utter surprise, you find that you both are back, together, in the Magical Place of Awareness standing by the Laurel Tree.

In a bit of shock, you find that you cannot speak. You look at your new friend and she starts to laugh with delight as she says, "You'll get used to this pretty soon! Miraculous experiences will continue to take place as you move forward on your exciting adventure. There are many Gifts and surprises ahead. Many shifts in consciousness and awareness as well"

You don't know what to say or do. Now you are truly speechless. Your thoughts are swirling. "What just happened? Did it actually happen?" Again, you wonder about the nature of reality, pondering, "Was the life I have been living actually an illusion of sorts. A dream—no a nightmare—I can choose to step out of?"

You have many more questions to ask, "If my decisions were made from unconscious urges and reactions then, no wonder my life isn't everything I would like it to be. What does she mean about shifts in consciousness. Does that have anything to do with what I have been perceiving?"

While still deep in thought, your attention is drawn back to the present. You turn back to her and she states, "As you gain greater awareness, you will start to feel better. You will start to have hope that maybe you can find what you are looking for. In time, you will discover your innate ability to create more of what you truly desire."

"Now that you have a greater understanding of the truth of what is taking place within yourself, hope will follow." As she utters these last words, she lifts her right arm and points ahead.

Your eyes follow, and a short distance away, you observe a two-story structure. The walls are pure glass. She continues, "This is where

I first heard the concepts that I have been sharing with you. Go there if your want to gain greater knowledge and clarity. I wish you well and would be delighted to see you again once you have taken more steps on your new path."

She embraces you and then takes leave. You feel such gratitude and are excited to see what awaits you. You look back to see her one more time and watch in disbelief as her body transmutes into a magnificent bright white light. Somehow, from deep inside, you can feel that much will be made known to you.

Appreciative of all that your new Team Member had just shared with you. You are inspired to immerse yourself in the same process. The confusion that had been a constant companion in your journey up to now is beginning to lift. What you just heard, really made sense. You are aware of how much it has already helped you to understand your inner world in a way that you never had before.

You realize that your False Voice made you believe that you could not do and have what was actually simply waiting for you to embrace. You now are coming to see that the power to create is yours. You can feel it flowing through your mind and body. Thankful for the incredible exchange, you continue heading in the direction of the structure.

You have a strong desire to reflect on the thoughts and beliefs that you hold and to learn where and when they originated. You make the decision that you will write them down in your special journal, whenever they arise. You are excited to add on to those already in your journal.

Moving through the forest, still in a bit of a daze, you are feeling revived and ready for whatever comes next. You have begun to expect the unexpected. The new awareness about the origins of beliefs makes you realize how much others people and your own past experiences have created the perspective that you have about life.

You now realize where your False Self, the one that was reflected back to you in the second cave, was formed. You realize that it is your False beliefs about yourself that are keeping it alive. You reflect on how wonderful it felt when you were connected to your True Self and have come to realize that you actually have the power to feel that more often. Into your consciousness, the realization of your own beauty is growing stronger.

A force is beginning to build within your being and you are determined to do whatever it takes to connect with your True Self. The desire and decision that you made at the beginning of your new journey is asserting itself. Now more than ever, you know that you will continue moving forward. But how?

The Glass Chalet

Still in deep reflection about your beliefs and how you acquired them, you notice that you are getting closer and closer to an absolutely beautiful glass structure. Approaching it and then peering through the windows, you can see some people inside. Curious and ready for whatever will come, you decide to enter, walking through the main doorway, wondering what is going on.

To your utter surprise and amazement, the building is brimming with lots and lots of people. As you continue to look around, you are blown away by the magnificence of the architecture. It appears as if some sort of training or teaching is taking place. You appreciate the architectural design which consciously integrates the chalet with the surrounding natural beauty of the forest. Thinking aloud, you hear yourself say, "What a remarkable achievement this is. It's so inspirational simply being in this breath-taking space."

As you wonder who the architect could be, your attention is drawn to a small group huddled together. Getting closer, you observe an old-fashioned blackboard with white chalk and an eraser. Written on the board is a note. This is what it says.

Dear Precious Student of Life,

Welcome to the SHIFT Training. Today, you will be studying various SHIFT Principles related to the inner workings of human beings. They are essential to living a conscious life. The Truths learned will raise your level of awareness and lead to a SHIFT, a new way of thinking, seeing and being. Enjoy yourself and the experience of becoming a student among many who are in the process of transforming their lives.

Congratulation on coming this far!!!

Your Professors

SHIFT Training

Location	Course Title	Speakers
Study Hall 1	Thoughts, Feelings and Behavior	Albert Ellis
Study Hall 2	Create Your Life Facilitator: Bonnie Barness	Albert Einstein Winston Churchill The Buddha
Meditation Hall	Precious Energy	Bonnie Barness

Reading the course offerings, you are quite intrigued. Not knowing where to go for the first lecture, you decide to follow a group people who look like they know where they are going. It appears that they do, because a sign inscribed with the words Study Hall One is coming into your field of vision. You enter behind them and find that the lecture has already begun.

At that moment, noticing your appearance, the professor stops, introduces himself as Albert Ellis and proceeds to shares his theory regarding how the words we say to ourselves, internally, relate to our feelings and our behaviors. He states that in this course, we will be looking at the relationship between thoughts and feelings. Your attention has definitely been captured.

The professor explains how what you think affects how you feel. As he shares his theory, you know that it is Truth. Your experiences in this Magical Place of Awareness has allowed you to see this direct correlation. You reflect back on your experiences in the caves and how the different words you heard were followed by powerful emotions.

You remember how wonderful you felt when the beautifully colored birds placed their positive words into the copper bowl and the nausea that overtook you when the crows dropped their toxic words into the other copper bowl. As you think back on these profound experiences and those under the Laurel Tree, you feel that unusual feeling inside of yourself again. The feeling that something powerful is happening within your entire being. The best way you are able to describe it is that everything seems to be shifting. You don't know what it is, other than it is real.

Deep in thought, your eyes glance around, looking out through the glass walls of the chalet. Thinking about how wonderful it is to be studying in such a beautiful environment, you feel gratitude and appreciation. You are aware these feelings, these wonderful warm feelings, came after a thought. It is the first time that, in the moment, you could see how this Principle is working within your own being. This realization is exhilarating and profound.

Your attention is drawn to the front of the room as the professor requests one of the students to come up to address the class. As the student reaches his destination, the professor introduces him as a former student who has come to talk with the new students. "When I first became aware of the relationship between thoughts and feelings, I was excited to apply the new knowledge into my life. I am here to share with you what happened."

"When I left the Magical Place of Awareness, the first time, I became extremely conscious of all of my thoughts. It was quite something, I can tell you. I had no idea previously how many thoughts I had throughout the day. As I began to pay close attention to my thoughts, I realized that there was an ongoing dialogue between my True Voice, which spoke words of support and encouragement, and my False Voice, filled with critical and judgmental comments."

It was amazing to actually observe this taking place. I noticed too, the close connection between my thoughts and emotions. It was one thing observing it here in the Magical

Place of Awareness; it was quite another when I could hear myself throughout the course of a day. It was overwhelming at times, but exciting too. I realized having this knowledge was going to change something in my life, I just didn't know what. But, boy, now I do!"

Thinking to yourself, "Wow, that's a lot to take in," you take a deep breath and continue to listen. "Sometimes, at the beginning, though, I would have difficulty knowing which Voice was talking. In order to be able to distinguish between the two voices, I really started paying attention to the emotions I was experiencing. I found that I always felt better when my True Voice was speaking."

One of the students raised his hand and asked, "How will I know which voice is loudest right now in my life ?" In response, the guest stated, "Simply ask yourself if you are usually happy and feel good about yourself or if you are often unhappy and feeling bad about yourself. Listen to your True Voice. What is it telling you? It knows the Truth."

The same student raises his hand and asks another question., "What happens if I cannot hear my True Voice?" The alumnus answers, "I used to ask myself the same question. As I listened closely, I could hear my True

Voice, but it was quite soft. I was grateful that I could hear it though, and had learned how to listen more intently in order to hear it more often."

"I came to understand, once I left this Magical Place of Awareness, about the volume settings on each of my voices. Therefore, in order to feel better, it was necessary to listen more for my True Voice and to believe it. Often I discovered it was so soft that I tended to disregard it or miss it all together because my False Voice came in so quickly and loudly. I noticed that having people in my life, my Support Team members who saw my True Self and expressed their appreciation for who I was, helped me hear my own True Voice."

"I used to think that I had to work at stopping my False Voice, but realized that it automatically becomes softer when I listened to my True Voice. Over time, I was able to noticed when my False Voice was speaking. I could identify it, hear the words spoken as critical and judgmental and then choose to listen to what was true, spoken by my True Voice. As this happened, my False Voice automatically became softer and over some time I didn't even know it was still there."

"That's what happened to me and it will happen to you, too. And when it does, self-doubt and fear will begin to diminish. Greater clarity and peace, will become yours. You will know that the first *SHIFT* has occurred once your True Voice becomes the loudest and strongest Voice within you."

You want to ask him about this *SHIFT,* but before you have a chance, another student raises her hand to ask a question. The teacher nods at her and she asks, "How will I be able to create change? It has always been my critical voice, my False Voice, that has pushed me to do something differently." The alumnus responds, "Most people have the belief that the only way that they can change a behavior that they do not want in themselves or in others is by being harsh and critical. This is what their False Self believes. I thought this, too."

"Since Experiencing the *SHIFT*, I am able to create the desired changes simply by listening to my True Voice and staying connected with my True Self, free from the inner suffering and pain. As you move forward on your new path, you will learn how to do the same. It is actually amazing how the whole thing works. I can't wait for you to experience it."

At that moment, you realize how hard you had been on yourself. Remembering all that you would say internally, your False Voice sitting in judgment, in order to make yourself do something that was challenging. Before having a chance to digest this new insight, the speaker continues, "I gained an even greater awareness of how vital it was to listen to my True Voice as I continued on my new path. I realized that the more that I listened to it, the more I was connected to my True Self and the happier I felt."

"I, also, gained a heightened awareness of how bad I felt about myself when I listened to my False Voice and how I would immediately disconnect from my True Self. I had another one of my many aha moments when I realized that throughout my life, it was this disconnection that had created a lot of my inner pain. This was the pain I frantically ran to numb. This Truth will become known to you as you begin to Experience the *SHIFT*."

You are stunned. It feels like an explosion is going off inside of your entire body and mind. In the midst of this inner upheaval, you ponder, "Did he just share with me one of the reasons why I am in so much emotional pain. Did he just explain that source of so much of the inner sufferings of all humankind?."

Before you can wrap your mind around this thought, the alumnus continues, "Our emotions speak to us. They let us know how we are feeling. To live consciously means being aware of how we are feeling and what we are thinking. The more aware we are of our feelings, the more alive we feel."

You realize that until right now, you had always thought that the emotional, psychological and existential pain you had experienced was caused by outside circumstances and other people. Now, with this new insight, you understand the source of some of your pain comes from within yourself.

With this new knowledge, you now reassert your decision, made on Second Step on your new path. From deep within you hear your True Voice speak loudly and clearly, "I am willing to do whatever it takes to be happy and no longer carry this terrible feeling inside of myself."

You understand that you have listened, in the past, to what others have said to you instead of listening to your own True Voice. You now understand that the reason you have been in so much pain is because you gave your power away to others by letting them tell you who you are and what you are capable of, instead of listening to your own True inner voice. You know that you have allowed yourself to believe in someone else's idea of who you are, instead, of listening to your own knowingness.

The alumnus continues, "Another way to recognize your True Voice is to remember the words that you have spoken when supporting a close friend that was in need of encouragement, appreciation or acknowledgment."

You are excited about this new insight. You know it will help you identify which voice is speaking from within in the future. "If my words are kind and compassionate, then I know it's my True Voice that I am hearing. If my words are mean and meant to cause pain, then I can be certain that my False Voice is coming out with a vengeance."

You decide to utilize this line of thinking to help determine which voice is speaking at the moment. You are acutely aware of how good it feels when your friend, through words of encouragement, helps you when you may be feeling down or insecure. You know how much better a friend feels when you do the same.

The graduate continues, "The words that you say to yourself about who you are significantly influence how you feel about yourself. When you put yourself down, it is the False Voice that is speaking. When you believe this voice, you begin to be disconnected from your True Self. Now, with your new awareness of the words spoken by both of your voices and how they impact the way you feel about yourself, you have taken an important step in changing the way that you feel within."

You notice your level of awareness growing as you think of various times when your thoughts affected how you were feeling and how different thoughts and words had the power to change your emotions and outlook.

The alumnus continues, "Now that you are more conscious, you can begin to choose which voice you want to listen to. You can feel better by choosing to listen to your True Voice more often. When you do so, you will be able to tap into your inner source of power. If you are not used to looking within, it may take some time."

"Though it may be confusing, initially, to distinguish between the two voices, know that in time, it will become much clearer to you. When this happens, confusion will be replaced with clarity on many different levels."

"Early on in my journey, I began getting into the practice of asking myself, 'What am I thinking? What am I feeling?' Some of my friends, also, called on their Support Team members to help them in their own personal endeavor to get in touch with their thoughts and feelings."

"Just as with all of us, in time your awareness will grow. At first, when you try to get in touch with your feelings, you may answer your questions by saying, 'I'm fine' or 'I'm good.' It is important to distinguish the various emotions and to use different and more specific adjectives to describe them."

As the speaker comes to a stop, the professor walks up to him, shakes his hand and thanks him for sharing what he had learned about the True Voice and False Voice with the class. He asks the alumnus if there are any parting words he would like to say. He nods his head and says, "In conclusion, I want to let you know that what I learned here, in this Magical Place of Awareness is at the foundation of all change and the *SHIFT*."

"I utilize the knowledge I am sharing with you each and every day. It has been essential to my ability to create the changes I have made in my life. The greater your awareness of your thoughts, the greater your ability to change your life and the world around you. I also found it useful to continue writing down my thoughts and associated feelings in my Experiencing the *SHIFT* Journal."

You are happy as you think, "I've already planned on doing that" and then the words pop into your head, "There I go again." You realize that you are aware again of how what you think affects how you feel. The alumnus concludes, "It helped me and I hope that it will help you too to gain a deeper understanding of what is actually taking place in your inner world, the world of thoughts and emotions."

"It was in this way that I gained the inner awareness I needed to create my life and my new way of being. I wish for you all the happiness that I have found on my new path. Thank you for listening as I shared with you a part of my journey. I hope that it will provide the knowledge and desire to continue moving forward on your new path!"

Knowing that you have learned an important Truth, you feel excited to find out what new insights will be gained in this incredible Glass Chalet. You notice that you are feeling so much less confused. You realize that the more aware you are of the two voices and the greater your ability to distinguish them from each other, the less overwhelmed and more equipped you will be to deal with life.

You look down at your journal thinking back to when you had fallen asleep under the

Laurel Tree. You start putting the pieces together, realizing how you have already gained so much awareness since entering this Magical Place of Awareness.

You are grateful that you had time to write down some of your thoughts and the corresponding emotions earlier in the journal and the corresponding emotions. It all makes a lot more sense to you now. You find that you want to know about the inner workings related to thoughts and feelings. You think, "The greater my awareness of how these two voices function, the greater will be my ability to create my own happiness."

As the alumnus goes to sit down with the other students, Ellis, the professor, continue to speak about the very important internal psychological system related to our thoughts, emotions and behaviors and how it works. He then thanks all of the students for being open to learning and growing. He reinforces how important it is that we are aware of what we say to ourselves if we want to create change in our lives.

You think to yourself, "This is the second time that thoughts and emotions have been tied together with behavior. I already have gained a rudimentary understanding of how thoughts and feelings are interconnected.

But I have no idea of how this relates to one's behavior." One of the students raises her hand to ask a question. She asks, "How should we apply this information into our lives?" You cannot believe it! She was thinking the same thing.

In the middle of her question, the teacher's assistant goes up to the front of the Study Hall and announces, "Our lecture is now over. There will be a forty-five minutes break. Please get ready to move on to Study Hall Number Two." He then looks at the student and states, "You will find part of your answer there." He wishes us well and directs us over to the Study Hall across on the other side of the building.

You walk out of the hall and into the lobby. There are so many different students here in this special place. Propelled by a strong desire to get more in touch with your thoughts and the feelings that follow, you take out your journal and look around in order find a comfortable place to contemplate. "That's the perfect place," you say aloud. You notice a window seat along the glass wall of the building. It looks so inviting. You walk over and plop yourself down, sinking into the soft feather-filled cushion.

With great anticipation, you turn to the page titled, CAVE ONE: YOUR TRUE SELF, reading what you had written down while in the wondrous cave a short time ago. Then you turn to the page, CAVE TWO: YOUR FALSE SELF. You look at the different thoughts inscribed in your journal, curious to discover their relationship to the past choices and previous actions taken.

You begin to write in your journal and are amazed at how the inner Principles are actually so real. Every time you had a negative, critical thought about yourself, you felt bad. And every time you had a positive, kind thought about yourself, you felt good. You can now see how what you have been saying to yourself has directly related to how you have been feeling. But how these feelings create your behaviors is news to you!

Deep in thought, you become aware that it has become a bit quieter. You look up and realize that there are only a few other students in the foyer. "Time certainly flies here!"

You rise to get ready to head to the next lecture, double-checking that all of your equipment is still securely placed in the toolbelt. Assured that everything is in its proper place as you place in the new journal, you realize that you are unsure where Study Hall Two is located. Observing a group of people walking together, you go over to ask if they know where it is.

"Come with us," one of the students said, "We're going there, too." On the way to the hall you learn that the next facilitator is actually the author of the book, the roadmap, you are carrying in your toolbelt. You wonder what you are going to hear as you enter the hall. Everyone is talking with great excitement about how, Albert Einstein, Winston Churchill and The Buddha are going to be making guest appearances.

As you are about to enter Study Hall Two, you remember how confused you had been earlier on in the day, and how challenging it was to distinguish the words coming from the True Voice and the False Voice. Now, with the knowledge acquired, you feel that you have the means to understand your inner self more than ever before.

What a concept! You realize that being conscious of your thoughts and feelings as much as possible is essential on your new path. You make the decision to be vigilant. You are excited about developing this new level of awareness.

Walking through the doorway, you can tell that the lecture is just about to begin. You, and those with you, quickly find seats. As you listen, it's as if the words sound just like they have jumped off the pages of your own book.

"Welcome. I would like to introduce myself to you. I am the author of your roadmap, Experiencing the *SHIFT*. I am so honored and thrilled that you are all here today."

"I know that you must have so many questions and I hope to answer some of them during our time together. Also, we are so incredibly blessed to have some brilliant and remarkable people with us who will share some of their wisdom with you as well."

"But first, I wish to help you gain a deeper understanding of Albert Ellis's theory regarding thoughts, emotions and behavior. There is an underlying principle of human behavior. Many great mystics in ancient civilizations and throughout the centuries have had knowledge of it."

"Here, in this Magical Place of Awareness, this wisdom is being passed on to you. It is one of the secrets of creating a wonderful life and I am so excited that you are at this point in your journey that you can receive it and then put it into practice." As you listen, you become aware of your surroundings. The facilitator is standing on a stage with a sheer white sheer curtain behind her. You wonder what is behind this veil. Your attention returns to the speaker.

"You now know that your feelings are directly related to what you think. You know, too, if you want to feel the joy and peace that is always within, it is necessary to take a look at your thoughts to see which ones lead to feelings of unworthiness, shame and guilt and which ones lead to feelings of joy and happiness."

"As human beings, though, we do not have any control over what thoughts come up in our mind, we do have the ability to choose which ones we will focus on and listen to. We, also, have the ability to choose which ones we will act upon."

"Beliefs are thoughts that are charged with intense emotion. You discovered, while under the LAUREL TREE, how many of your beliefs were created. Your past actions were based on the these beliefs though you may not have been aware at the time. The life that you have right now was created, for the most part, by the thoughts and beliefs you chose to act upon. If you want to feel a greater sense of well-being, change some of your thoughts."

"Most people are not aware they have this ability. Their thoughts arise and then they react with words or actions to the internal emotions. When unpleasant or painful emotions are experienced, often they will numb them with alcohol, drugs, food or other activities like sex, gambling, vaping, and excessive work or physical activity. You do have the ability to choose which thoughts you put your attention on and which you will not. This choice, in turn, determines to a great degree how you will feel, the actions you will take and the quality of your life."

"From your experiences in this Magical Place of Awareness, you know the powerful effects your thoughts have on how you feel. Every decision that you have made in your life and that you are making right now is based on your thoughts and feelings. In the past, if you were not aware, unconscious, of what your were thinking, your actions were not completely in your control. The greater your awareness of your thoughts and feelings, the greater your ability to create the life that you desire."

You are beginning to realize how the numbing of your thoughts and feelings has interfered with this ability. You have an inner knowing that once you reflect on some of your past choices and remember the thoughts and feelings that lead to those decisions, much clarity will be gained. "I really need time by myself," you ponder, "so that I can think about this a lot more. Maybe after the class, if there is time, I'll use my journal to process this more. Right now, I want to listen."

You notice someone a couple of rows in front of you, somewhat hesitantly, raise his hand. The facilitator stops speaking in order to listen to the question about to be asked. "This is quite difficult for me to talk about, but I know how important it is that I am honest with myself and open up in order to gain greater awareness and understanding."

"I have a number of addictive behaviors that started when I was in college. They often go hand-in -hand. I will drink alcohol which then leads to using cocaine or some other drug. I feel free and happy at the moment and enjoy myself while gambling, having sex, or eating everything that I desire. At those times, I feel like I don't have a care in the world. It is a wonderful escape from my thoughts and the reality of my life, even if it is temporary."

"The only problem is that lately, it doesn't seem to be working as well. I find that I am not enjoying myself as in the past and the day after, well, that has always been miserable. I have wanted to stop these behaviors and sometimes can for awhile, but then it is as if I lose all control and they take over again. It has become a vicious cycle and now I am in even more pain than before."

"This lifestyle has, increasingly over time, begun to effect all of my relationships. Now it is even starting to interfere with the quality of my work and health. I can't stand how I lie to people to cover all of this up. The feelings of guilt and shame are so overwhelming at time that I don't know what to do. I feel so terrible about myself."

"I stepped onto my new path because I want so much more from life and I have made the decision to do whatever it takes to be free of this pain. I don't know how that will happen. It's almost too hard to believe that it is possible. Whatever you can share that might give me a better understanding of what I have been going through would be so very much appreciated. Thank you."

All eyes turn to the front of the room wondering what is going to happen next. The speaker, Bonnie Barness, begins. "Thank YOU so much for sharing what has been heavy on your heart. Know that by doing so, you are giving words to thoughts and feelings many of the individuals have here today. All of us feel pain. If we do not get relief from within, we look without to wherever we can find it. Sometimes we get the relief we so desperately want, but realize that it is sadly only temporary."

"As we continue taking these actions, eventually, more pain follows along with despair, feelings of guilt and shame as well as a sense of hopelessness. The process of disconnection that began when we were younger, which is the source of much of the pain even though it may not seem to be the case, continues and escalates. There seems to be no way out."

"The wonderful news is there is a way out of the pain. The path, which you are now on, is one of freedom; freedom from guilt, anxiety and shame; freedom from the past; freedom to choose, to choose your actions instead of having the emotion, substance or activity have control over you."

Another student raises her hand and asks, "How can something or someone have control over you?" The facilitator responds. "Certain substances have an addictive quality. Once you have crossed the line, you are now aware exists, neurobiological changes which have occurred within your brain create this irrepressible urge. There are also emotional, psychological, and behavioral components as well. After many years of numbing the inner pain with substances or certain behaviors, it becomes an automatic, unconscious response."

"All addictive substance, including sugar, have the powerful effect of activating the reward system in the brain. This effect accounts for the intensely pleasurable feelings that most people experience initially. Overtime, with increased use, changes can occur in the structure and function of the brain."

"These changes, neuroadaptations, drive the transition from controlled, occasional substance use to chronic misuse, which can become more difficult to control. Moreover, these brain changes can endure long after an individual stops using."

You think to yourself, "I know people that drank and used throughout college, but afterwards still had the ability to choose." As if hearing your thoughts, the speaker continues, "However, addiction is not an inevitable consequence of substance use."

"Whether initial use progresses into an addiction depends on many factors including genetic makeup and other biological factors, personality and psychological factors, the age when the person started using and the environment in which they live. Supported scientific evidence shows that these changes in the brain persist long after substance use stops. It is not yet known how much these changes may be reversed or how long that process may take."

You are stunned. You always thought that your inability to limit or stop the intake of alcohol and drugs over a prolonged period of time was due to a lack of willpower. You had always thought there was something wrong with you, that you were simply weak and something was inherently lacking in your character.

Hearing there is actually a neurobiological component related to the challenges experienced in the past is incredible and truly eye-opening. You have so many questions. You want, need, to know more. You raise your hand and the facilitator responds.

"I see we have another person with a question." She points to me and I begin, "Could you share more about the changes in the brain that you were discussing and the behavioral changes as well?" She smiles and continues. "It is my pleasure. There is well-supported scientific evidence which shows that addiction to various substances is due to a disruption in three different areas of the brain. It also suggests that the addiction process involves a three-stage cycle: bing/intoxication, withdrawal/negative affect and preoccupation/anticipation."

"Boy, do I know that cycle well," you think to yourself. She continues, "With continuous use, this cycle becomes more severe overtime. The disruption can create dramatic changes in brain function. This in turn makes it more difficult for a person to control his or her substance use."

"When this disruption occurs, substance-associated cues- like people, activities and the substance itself-can trigger substance seeking behaviors. A reduction in the brain systems sensitivity can effects the experience of pleasure reward. The person will then have a need for more of the substance to feel the same pleasure. This often leads to an increase in consumption or use. A reduction of the brain executive control systems, involved in the ability to make decisions and regulate one's actions, emotions and impulses, can lead to a decrease in the ability to control one's behaviors and actions."

The woman next to you begins to squirm. She raises her hand and lets out an uncomfortable laugh. The facilitator looks in her direction and asks if she has a question. In response, she begins to speak. "As I am listening to everything you are sharing about how certain substances at some point can take control of a person's actions and behaviors, I know that feeling, but it isn't related to something, but rather to someone." She takes a deep breath and continues.

"I have felt that urge, irresistible urge, to call someone that I know is unhealthy for me, but I do it anyways. Many times in the past, I may have ended the relationship only finding myself almost begging for the person to want me, to give me the love and attention that I am craving, to see me again. The feeling of loneliness engulfs me. Why is this cycle so much like the one you are discussing with us about certain substances?"

All eyes turn to the stage. The author smiles a knowing and compassionate smile. With kindness in her eyes, she begins. "I know how much this feeling you describe feels like love, but it is not. Rather, it comes from a need to numb pain from the past, pain from your own disconnection with your True Self, pain that comes from not giving yourself what you need in the present to fulfill your physical, mental, emotional, spiritual needs. This is the same pain that others may use food, alcohol, cigarettes, video games, gambling and other normally healthy activities done in excess to escape."

"On your new path, as you heal and receive your many Gifts, you will be able to give to yourself what you need to be happy and fulfilled. Instead of reaching towards people who do not treat you the way that you deserve, you will only bring in people who do."

"Once you truly love yourself, you will not need to find it from others, realizing that you have it all within. You will find yourself choosing to love and be loved by those who actually can." Whoa. This is mind-boggling. I really have to let this in. Do I do this? Hmmm. This is something I want to think about...later!"

She continues, "Here on your new path, you will discover how to process your painful emotions and then release them. Instead of pushing down the pain for it to simply re-emerge whenever you least expect it, you will, instead, address the pain in the moment."

"Through this process of *SHIFT* Actualization™, you will attain much knowledge of yourself, the people around you and of life itself. The knowledge and these insights will allow for a different way of thinking, seeing and being. Wonderful adventures of self-actualization and transformation are just waiting for you!"

"With the new awareness gained here on your new path, you will acquire a different perspective on the actions people are taking and the situation unfolding. You will be aware of what is happening within your own being, your thought, emotions and beliefs. This will open up new possibilities, new ways of seeing, thinking, and being. Your thoughts and feelings about what is occurring will often be different due to your ability to observe the situation from a higher vantage point."

"In place of intense pain, will be greater understanding. In place of feeling powerless, to stop the pain and unwanted behaviors, will be the realization that you have the ability to look at a situation through a different lens."

"With the insights and knowledge gained along the path, this new way of seeing will lead to a new way of thinking about what is occurring and a new way of being in how you feel and respond to the situation at hand." The first questioner raises his hand again. His face is filled with pain, but his eyes convey a small gleam of hope. "Is this possible for me? Can I really be in the world in a new way? Can the urge really go away?"

"Along your new path, the possibility is available for you to gain many insights, Gifts and Manifesting Charms. You can, then, apply what you have acquired to the various situations that arise. As you do so, feelings of powerless begin to lessens and so does the urge. Pain will be replaced by feelings of joy and peace, feelings that you may not have felt for a very long time."

"As you continue to connect more and more with your True Self, you will come to realize who you thought you were, the False Self, is false. The inner suffering created from the words spoken by your False Voice will be replaced with feels of gratitude and appreciation for the beautiful person that you are."

"You will begin to identify the people, places and circumstances where the urge has taken control in the past. You will get in touch with what you need and begin giving it to yourself. You will take care of yourself through the choices you make.

Some people you will eliminate from your life. Some people you will bring closer. The wounds will start to heal and the urge to go away. The Gifts and Manifesting Charms you receive will provide the means to experience fulfillment and love on a much deeper level."

The author concludes, "The accumulation of each new choice and action you will make, as you go forward on your path will begin to create the life you will have. As you *SHIFT*, connecting more and more with your True Self, hearing your True Voice, feelings of enthusiasm, gratitude and confidence, will get stronger. As you do so, feelings of powerless will begin to lessen and so will the urge."

"When your words, actions and choices are in alignment your True Self, your life will begin to reflect more of who you truly are.

Clarity and self-respect will take the place of disconnection and confusion. Inner peace and tranquility will be your to have. Know that it all begins with connecting with your True Self." Wow, you whisper under your breath. Again, I am blown away. Maybe my dream can really come true.

You hear the authors voice ringing like a crystal bell through the hall, "I now have the honor of inviting the distinguished panel of speakers onto the stage. Each has impacted those during his lifetime and for many, many generations that have followed. Whether it was through religion, politics or science, their wisdom has had a profound effect. We are so grateful to have them here with us in this Magical Place of Awareness."

As if by some unseen force, the curtain is drawn back and on the stage are a number of comfortable armchairs placed in a semi-circle. Your eyes are glued ahead anxiously waiting for the first guest to appear. You cannot believe it. Right there, in front of you, walking onto the stage is the Buddha. You rub your eyes. You know it cannot be, though, it had been written in plain sight on the blackboard at the entrance of the Glass Chalet. The Buddha continues to cross the stage until he is directly in the center.

The facilitator, Bonnie Barness, goes up to him and begins to speak, "We are so honored to have you hear today to address these students of Truth. They have made the decision and have taken the first steps on their new path. Here in this Magical Place of Awareness, they have started to become conscious of who they truly are. Today, we would be grateful, to hear the wisdom that you have that can support them as they move forward on their journey."

The Buddha bows down, they both take their seats facing one another and the Buddha begins to speak, "All that we are is a result of what we have thought. The mind is everything. What you think, you become. All that we are is the result of what we have thought. It is founded on our thoughts and made up of our thoughts."

"Oh, my", you hear yourself exclaim aloud. You realize that what you are learning in this Magical Place of Awareness has been around for a very long time. You hear yourself thinking, "If this is so than why doesn't anyone know about this or talk about this?"

You find that you don't have the answer. You look up towards the stage and hear the facilitator speak, "Thank you for sharing with us this great Truth. We are fortunate to have another man of great distinction, he is British in fact, joining us here in our discussion. I would like to bring him, now, out onto the stage. Mr. Winston Churchill, will you please present yourself."

In amazement, you watch as Winston Churchill emerges from the wings. He turns to the audience and then finds an empty seat and sits firmly down. The room is silent. "Welcome Mr. Churchill. I am so honored that you can be here with us today. I believe that you have knowledge of the Buddha and his teachings. He has honored us as well with his presence."

"Today, we have speaking with the students who are in search of happiness and Truth, about the power of thoughts and how they effect our emotions and actions. I have shared some of my own knowledge with them on the subject as well. I believe that we come into this world as a beautiful Soul and through the choices we make, we create who we become in the world."

"The choices we have made in the past have created much of what our lives are right now. These choices were based largely on our thoughts and feelings. The choices we make today and in the days to come will also be made based on what we think and feel now and in the future."

"The students of life are now coming to understand that through introspection, they can begin to have greater knowledge of past thoughts and actions which have lead to positive outcomes in their lives and positive feelings about themselves and which ones have not. For many, this is new knowledge."

"I was wondering if you could honor us with your thoughts are on this matter?" Winston responds. "Man occasionally stumbles over truth, but most pick themselves up and hurry off as if nothing happened. I believe that every man should ask himself each day whether he is not too readily accepting of negative solutions. This is so important because I believe that you create your own universe as you go along."

The author thanks Mr. Churchill and then turns to the students. She says, "I have found the same to be true and there is another guest here today, a brilliant scientist, that has come onto this Truth as well. May I introduce Albert Einstein."

There, right in front of your eyes, walks out Albert Einstein. He looks just like the photos that you have seen of him. You are so excited. You feel so blessed to be in the presence of such distinguished guests.

After greeting the other members of the panel, he sits in the last empty seat on the stage. The author addresses him and says, "We have been discussing the power of thought to create our reality. Mr. Churchill was just saying..." Churchill jumps in, "...You create your own universe as you go along." The Buddha adds, "I have found that nothing can harm you as much as your own thoughts unguarded." The facilitator joins in, "Yes, the students have been learning about the power of their False Voice and how much pain comes from listening and acting on the words it speaks."

Turning again to Mr. Einstein, she asks him what he thinks about these ideas. He pauses, placing his fingertips together. It is so quiet that you could hear a pin drop. Then he begins, "The world as we created it is a process of our thinking. It cannot be changed without changing our thinking."

The author responds, "Yes. Mr. Einstein. Not only is one person's life changed by the process of his or her thoughts, but actually all of humankind creates the world that we live in by these thoughts as well."

"We, all, have created the world that we have by the thoughts that we have chosen to act upon. If we, within each society, choose to act upon thoughts that lead to happiness, peace and fulfillment the world would be a very different place than it is now."

The scientist continues, "You cannot solve problems with the same level of consciousness that created them." With great optimism, he turns to the students and says, "One moment can change a day, one day can change a life and a life can change the world." With that he becomes quiet.

The facilitator looks out to the students and continues, "Through this process of transformation that is occurring as you move forward on your new path, you are gaining great awareness and are moving to higher levels of consciousness."

"As new challenges arise, you will become aware of options and possibilities unseen of in the past. These options, when chosen, will lead to different outcomes. You will then Experience the *SHIFT*, living in the same world, but everything will feel different due your new knowledge, perspective and actions. You will begin to go through life with a new way of seeing, thinking and being."

"Our honored guests have all experienced the *SHIFT* and have lived their lives from this higher level of conscious awareness. The way they think and the choices that they have made have had a huge impact on those during their lifetimes and for many, many generations until today."

"You, each one of you, have the power to go to new levels of awareness and higher levels of consciousness. Each of you have the ability to connect with your own True Self and create a life filled with inner peace, harmony and joy."

"The peace that you seek is within you at all times. It is what you feel when you are connected with your Soul, your True Self. Awaken to this Truth. No matter what is happening around you, you have the ability to stay connected. Choose your thoughts wisely. Let you thoughts and actions reflect your True Self. Actualize your True Self in the world. It is your purpose. It is your destiny."

As the author, returns to her seat, Albert Einsteins speaks. It is almost inaudible. "There isn't enough darkness in the world to snuff out the light of one little candle." She notices the Buddha. He is sitting,with his eyes shut, in a lotus position. He appears to be in a state of mediation. Sensing that he is being observed, he opens his eyes. The facilitator asks him to describe what he was experiencing and if there is anything that he wishes to share with the students.

He begins, "Peace comes from within. Do not seek it without." He then begins to encourage the students to utilize the awareness they have gained, here, in the Magical Place of Awareness, as they move forward on their new path. Talking to them in the third person, he goes on, "His mind becomes calm. His word and deed are calm. Such is the state of tranquility of one who has attained to deliverance through the realization of Truth."

You observe that he has returned to a deep state if meditation. He continues, as if the information is being channeled through him to those in the hall. "No one saves us, but ourselves. No one can and no one may. We must walk the path alone. If you propose to speak, always ask yourself, is it true, is it necessary is it kind? However many holy words you read, however many you speak, what good will they do you if you do not act upon them? An idea that is developed, put into action, is more important than an idea that exists only as an idea."

You find that you are just taking all of this in. Here in the Study Hall you have been hearing a lot about Truth. You are becoming aware that great Truths are at the foundation of the new path you are on. From what you have been learning and from what the Buddha has just shared, you now understand that by listening to your True Voice and being connected to your True Self a sense of calmness and tranquility occurs.

You are stunned at how profound this journey has already been. Again, the thought goes through your head, "I had no idea when I started on my new path what a journey I was undertaking." You feel grateful that you discovered this new path and turn your attention to those on the stage giving so generously if their time and wisdom.

The facilitator turns to the guests and begins. "We are now coming to the end of our time together. I would like to ask each of you, before you go, if there is anything that you would like to say to the students here as they get ready to continue forward on their new path." She turns to Winston Churchill. He stands up and walks almost to the edge of the stage peering out into the audience.

"Its wonderful," he starts out, "what great strides can be made when there is a resolute purpose behind them. No one saves us, but ourselves. No one can and no one may. We ourselves must walk the path. The only two mistakes one can make along the road to Truth, not going all the way."

"Continuous effort—not strength or intelligence—is the key to unlocking our potential. Courage is rightly esteemed the first of human qualities because it has been said, it is the quality which guarantees all the others. If you are facing in the right direction, all you need to do is keep walking."

He continues to share the wisdom that he had gained throughout his lifetime, "It is better to conquer yourself than to win a thousand battles. The victory is yours. It cannot be take from you. Those who have failed to work towards the Truth have missed the purpose of living."

"Everyday you make progress. Every step may be fruitful, yet there will stretch out before you an ever-lengthening, ever-ascending, ever-improving path. You know you will never get to the end of the journey. But this, so far from discouraging, only adds to the joy and glory of the climb." Wishing the students lots of luck and courage, he walks off the stage.

You look around, almost expecting everyone to clap. You hear nothing, but feel a sense of great humility as you look at the faces of the students around you. At that moment, you realized how many others, just like you, are starting out on their new path. You feel chills as you sense how deeply they, too, are being effected by the words that have been shared and the profound experience here in the study hall.

The author then turns to Albert Einstein. He looks at her and then to the student and begins to make his final remarks, sharing what he believed was essential for him to have done in his lifetime." I realized that I must be willing to give up what I am in order to become what I will be. I came to understand that the measure of intelligence is the ability to change, any fool can know. The point is to understand. I have come to see and know that reality is merely an illusion, albeit a very persistent one and that imagination is everything. It is the preview of life's coming attractions."

He instructed the students, "The important thing is not to stop questioning. Curiosity has its own reason for existence. One cannot help but be in awe when he contemplates the mysteries of eternity, of life, of the marvelous structure of reality. It is enough if one tries merely to comprehend a little of the mystery each day." And with those last words of wisdom, he bids the students farewell and exits to the wings of the stage.

Before you have a chance to catch your breath, you can feel all around you a hum. Everyone is focused on the Buddha in anticipation of what he will say. As if feeling their energy, he opens his eyes and bows. Standing up from his lotus position, he speaks, "Awakening isn't the end. It is the beginning. Every morning we are born again. What we do today is what matters" and then he walk off the stage.

Complete silence permeates the room. It is palatable. There is something powerful going on, yet nothing physically has changed. All eyes move towards the author. After a few moments, she slowly stands up and then speaks.

"Today is the first day of the rest of your life. It is your choice how you live it. We have all been honored by the presence of those who have came before us and with us here today. Take what they have shared, as will I, to heart and let it support you and guide you in your journey ahead."

"Know that you are on your new path. The *SHIFT* has already begun to happen. It takes courage to look within. Know that you deserve all the gifts that life has to offer. Now is the time. This is the moment to begin to actualize your True Self in the world. Choose your thought and actions wisely. What do you want to create? The choice is yours to make."With those last words, she too, leaves the stage.

The room is so still, so quiet. Then, a buzz commences spreading through the hall. Everyone is looking at each other. Some stand up and begin walking towards the doorway. Others begin to follow. Everyone appears quite stunned, yet exhilarated. You rise and begin to leave the hall, too. It feels as if your feet are not quite touching the ground.

Crossing the threshold, you feel something sort of funny inside your torso. At first, you are a bit alarmed until you realize that it is the same sensation that you felt earlier out in the forest. You laugh aloud as you realize that it is your inner scale and you can actually feel it moving

You are tickled to think that you are able to be in touch with your feelings. Usually, in the past, if you felt something uncomfortable, you would just push it down and keep doing whatever you were doing. Now, you want to feel. You want to know what is going on within.

You realize that this scale has been inside most of your life. You understand, even more than ever, the importance of looking at each of the words and statements in your own copper bowls in order to create, first, an internal change. You no longer want to listen to words coming from the False Self that the crows brought in. You want your scale to *SHIFT*.

You know this has already begun to happen. You are determined to become aware of all you thoughts and feelings. You know that you are willing and have the courage to look at the behaviors and choices previously made along with their related outcomes.

Reflecting on some of the thoughts and words that you had inscribed earlier in your journal, you now think about the behaviors and circumstances that followed each one. You are absolutely amazed at how the words spoken by your True Voice, so often, led to healthy interactions and how the thoughts coming from your False Voice led to unhealthy behaviors and undesirable events. You can see so clearly the direct correlation between your thoughts and what followed.

You recognize that when your actions were based on the words spoken from your True Self, you felt great and your actions were a reflection of your authentic Self. You also realize that when you actions and behaviors were based on the words spoken by you False Voice, you felt terrible and your actions were not in alignment or a reflection of who you know you truly are. You can see now how these thoughts had led to certain behaviors that did not support your well-being.

The past confusion continues to lift as you remember the terrible things that you had said to yourself, noticing how feelings of worthlessness arose followed by self-destructive and self-defeating behaviors. Numerous other examples flood your mind as the connections become clearer and clearer.

You begin to feel quite overwhelmed. Thinking, "Now that I have this new level of awareness what do I do?" In a daze, yet feeling such a sense of elation, you overhear the students right in front of you asking each other where they are suppose to go next. They are talking about finding the Meditation Hall. "That sounds just like what I can use right now," you hear yourself say softly under your breath.

Somehow, without realizing it, your unconscious thoughts and their accompanying emotions propel action and you find yourself walking over to the posted schedule to see where the Meditation Hall is located. You read, now, that the next class is upstairs. You hadn't noticed a stairway and actually only thought that it was a one-story building. Heading back towards the study halls, you notice a spiral staircase off to the side. "Hmmm. That's a bit odd," you think, wondering why you hadn't see it before.

As you look up the staircase, it appeared to lead up to some sort of loft. You walk towards it and begin to climb. As you do so you are a bit surprised that there aren't any other students going up as well. "Rather odd," you remark aloud.

As you continue to climb, you experience the unusual sensation of being inside and outside at the same time. You think it is because of the glass windows. Spaces blur into one. It's as if something is shifting within yourself and at the same time your outside reality seems to be shifting as well. You are feeling warm and a bit happy.

Applying what you have just learned, you realize that you are actually hearing your True Voice and are feeling good. You can feel the scale tipping as more of the kind, supportive words are getting louder and growing in number. As this is happening, you can sense that the critical words are getting softer and that side of the scale is becoming lighter. "Wow. This stuff really works!"

Reaching the top, you are met by a girl dressed all in white. As you begin to speak to her, she place her index finger to her lips and silently begins to walk toward a closed door, a number of feet ahead, indicating that you should follow. You feel like you are in a tree house with grand, very ancient trees all around.

She opens a door and leads you in a large room with mats on the ground. Up in the front, you can see a man, also, dressed in white, sitting in the lotus position. She points for you to go to the front of the room and closes the door behind her as she leaves.

It is very quiet. You notice the energetic vibration pulsating just so slightly. Again, you find it unusual that no one else is there. You assumed that a large number of students would be attending as in the previous classes. You progress slowly across the room and lower yourself onto the mat in front of the seated man. He has a very long white beard and appears deep in meditation. You are not sure what to do next, but you decide to just wait.

The quiet is soothing after all that you have been through. There is a coolness is in the air that is refreshing, yet calming. You close your eyes and rest. It feels so good. No thoughts. No emotions. Just peace. Light. Calm.

Hours pass...so it seems. Then, as if wakening within this dream-state, you find yourself floating out in the universe. You can see the stars around you. Feeling weightless and free, you begin to feel energy from this universe, swirling around you. It enter through your body. Surging through and all around you. You can feel your energy soar.

At that moment, a figure appears. He seems familiar to you. And then it hits you. Sitting right in front of you is the Buddha. How can this be? The energy stops whirling and everything becomes still. A bit confused, you ask him if you are dreaming. He only smiles. He then begins to talk, "Everything is energy. You are energy. Energy creates. It is the force behind creation. Your energy creates your world. Emotion is energy that gives thoughts focus and the ability to create new realities."

Time passes. Clouds float towards you. As you watch, they spread apart as a huge book breaks through. To your delight, you realize it is your special roadmap, Experiencing the *SHIFT*. The words begin to move towards you, as if with a life of their own and speak. "You have energy and it is precious because it is yours. Your Precious Energy is available to create your life, within the physical reality, and is finite. Use it wisely."

All of a sudden everything seemed to come together and make sense. The new thoughts and emotions that you have experienced here in the Magical Place of Awareness have opened your eyes to the secret to creating a life that truly reflects your True Self.

You realize that this new awareness is giving you another key to life. You embrace the gift of life and choose to make a difference in the lives of others. It is your Soul's purpose to manifest and actualize your own unique beauty in the world. You have your Precious Energy available to express and create, through your thoughts, emotions and actions, a life filled with peace joy and meaning. Somehow, as if from a far distance away, you hear a few last spoken words, "Choose Wisely."

You abruptly awaken. In front of you is the same old man that was in your dream. Or was it a dream? Was it real? You began to wonder, again, what is real and what is not. How you used to think and believe doesn't hold true for you any longer. It feels like a *SHIFT* has occurred in your worldview and perception of yourself. New truths have been revealed.

As you stand up, you feel a bit shaky. Your legs do not seem to be holding you up as well as before. As you turn to leave you whisper, "thank you" and walk backwards towards the door. A feeling of great respect is not allowing you to turn your back towards the meditative man. Once at the door, you bow your head and leave the room.

You feel a blessing upon your head. You are overwhelmed with humility and gratitude as you realize that you have just been in the presence of something more powerful than you have ever experienced. You close the door behind you, heading back to the staircase.

Half expecting to see the girl, you begin down the flight without an encounter. You walk to the front door, knowing that you have completed all that was on the schedule for the day. You feel as if you are walking on a cloud.

You move through the large foyer and as you are about go out the front door, you turn around to double-check that nothing else has been added to the schedule and are surprised at what you see. Only two classes are listed. The first in Study Hall Number One and the other in Study Hall Number Two. Nothing is written regarding the Meditation Room.

You are stunned, For a second, you question your own sanity. "Is my mind playing tricks on me? What is real? What is illusion? What is going on?" You look back towards where you just came. Amazed, but not really, the spiral staircase and loft have both disappeared.

As you step across the threshold and back into the forest, you are stuck with a thought.

It actually feels physical. You hear from within, from your True Voice, "You are a jewel. You are precious. You are divine." You now know this is true.

Feeling as if you are floating amongst the tall, ancient trees, you are surprised when you notice the sun setting on the horizon. Time seems to be allusive here. You can feel the energy of the sun as you walk outside. You feel its warmth connect with your own energy, feeling a tremendous power surge through you. From deep within you hear, "Your energy is precious because it is yours. It is here for you to create the life you desire as you take the next steps on your new path."

You feel your Precious Energy soaring through your entire body. It feels so wonderful. Your consciousness is expanding. Your awareness growing. You now realize that, just as you have the ability to choose your thoughts, you also have the ability to choose where and how you will use your Precious Energy.

You are excited to discover how the new awareness will add to the *SHIFT* you are beginning to experience. You want this feeling to last forever. So much is changing and so quickly. You are feeling so much better, somehow so different, than before starting on your journey. You love this special place and want to spend more time in its warm embrace, but you sense from deep within that it is time to go.

Jimminy

As you find yourself being drawn back in the direction from which you had first entered into this Magical Place of Awareness, you notice how the colors of the sunset are more beautiful than those in any painting or photograph you have ever seen. You can feel your energy flowing, strong and vibrant.

You hear coming from within, "The knowledge given to me, here, has provided a new foundation upon which to build my life. The great Truths revealed have provided powerful insights about myself. I have been given a key that will open the door to the unknown, filled with more freedom, meaning and purpose than I could have even dreamed possible."

Up ahead, you can see the pond and beyond it the ancient red gateway, just as it appeared in your ancient scroll. You feel the subtle, yet powerful change which has taken place within yourself since first arriving in this magical place. As you walk over to the pond, something catches your eye. Bending down to take a closer look, you notice a reflection of yourself smiling back, surrounded by a beautiful white light.

You are mesmerized. You know that you are no longer the same. As you look up, you can see that the boulder has shifted as well. It's as if the boulder is reflecting the internal changes that have taken place within your own being. The confusion you had at the beginning of your journey is lifting and in its place a clearer vision is emerging.

The *SHIFT*, you can feel it, is taking place on the deepest possible level of your being. You know the paradigm of life and yourself, you held for so many years is shifting, too. Each experience in the Magical Place of Awareness has led to a new way of thinking and seeing. You are excited to continue on your path towards a new way of being, towards the freedom you so greatly desire; Freedom from Addiction. Freedom to be You.

As you turn to head out in the direction of the magical red gateway, you are startled. Right on your shoulder appears something quite spectacular! To your utter surprise, he begins to talk! He introduces himself to you as Jimminy and announces that it is a VERY important member of your support team. You think, "He certainly is connected with his True Self."

Before you have a chance to respond, he states his purpose. "I am Jimminy, or you may know me by another name, and am here to help you stay aware and conscious at every moment. I can take any shape that you wish."

"Living consciously is essential to creating the freedom you desire and a life that reflects your unique and amazing True Self. I will remained perched on your shoulder throughout your journey, on the lookout for you, helping you to implement the changes in your life you choose to make and to support you in manifesting your many powerful and exciting dreams."

You are speechless. Jimminy continues, "Awareness is the first key to change. It is what moves you forward on this path. It is they key that opens up the door to your new life. As you have come to know, the new awareness gained has allowed you to begin to see yourself, your life, your actions, and relationships in a whole new light."

"While so often in the past, you responded to events based on unconscious thoughts and beliefs, you now have the ability to become more aware moment to moment, making choices from this higher vantage point. With each step, you will gain additional insights into yourself and into the life that you have created."

"Knowledge is power and the more knowledge you have of the underlying principals and truths about yourself, human behavior about how life works, the greater you ability to create a wonderful present and future."

"A paradigm *SHIFT* has already started to happen. With greater awareness comes greater understanding . It is this underlying ingredient which is involved in growth on all levels. A shift in consciousness occurs once a certain level of awareness has been reached. Awareness is the key."

Approaching the gate, you feel a tingly sensation. You are excited about what is to come. You turn your head to make sure that Jimminy is still perched on your shoulder, there to help you stay conscious of all the knowledge and insights you have already gained.

As you do so, you hear your new companion whisper something into your ear. As you listened oh so closely, you hear him say, "Have no fear. Jimminy is here." Together you enter into the cloud, excited about the new adventure that awaits you.

You feel something within moving and smile, knowing this now wonderfully familiar feeling of your inner scale shifting, With your toolbelt comfortably hugging your hips, connected with your True Self, you are ready for the amazing journey ahead.

From deep within, you feel your Precious Energy surge through you, propelling you forward on your new path. You feel yourself moving towards a higher level of consciousness. You want with all of your heart and soul to Experience the *SHIFT* into a new way of thinking, seeing and being.

YOU TAKE YOUR NEXT STEP.

ABOUT THE
Author

Bonnie Barness is from Beverly Hills, California and is a graduate of UCLA She currently resides in Scottsdale, Arizona, where she maintains a private practice providing psychotherapy, hypnotherapy, Intuitive Therapy and *SHIFT* AP™ Coaching.

Ms. Barness has created the *SHIFT* Actualization Process™, *SHIFT* AP™, in which individuals are able to *SHIFT* out of pain, blocks, barriers, and limitations into a new state of consciousness, allowing for a greater experience of joy, happiness, fulfillment and the manifestation of dreams.

Organizations and businesses can Experience The *SHIFT* in its internal culture. Collaboration, team work and a fresh and innovative approach to conflict resolution and development of emotional intelligence on a whole new level.

Utilizing powerful wisdom and knowledge leading to great success and an inspirational workplace. Freedom From Addiction program available, including Executive *SHIFT* AP™ Coaching, utilizing this innovative new and exciting process.

This accelerated process of transformation can be experienced through individual and groups sessions. It is offered in the workplace, virtually, in clinics and retreats. Training is available to become a *SHIFT* AP™ Facilitator and Coach in your workplace or private business. Opportunities to become a *SHIFT* AP™ Sales Representative are available as well.

As an writer and speaker, Ms. Barness enjoys sharing her unique approach to personal and workplace relationships, life and spiritual growth with others. On radio, television, social media, podcasts and as an expert source for the Arizona Republic and in her advice column,"Ask Bonnie", she has provided specific strategies for dealing with life's challenges, for living life to its fullest and to experience powerful, spiritual awakenings and transformation.

For more information, please visit BonnieBarness.com or
email BonnieBarness@yahoo.com.

GET READY FOR THE NEXT STEPS ON YOUR *New Path!*

Knowing that you want more. Having made the decision to do whatever it takes to have the joy and happiness that you desire with all of your being. You started on your new path! You have your Toolbelt comfortably hugging your hips and have experienced all of the wonders in the Magical Place of Awareness.

The *SHIFT* has already begun. With the new knowledge and awareness you have gained, you are now ready to continue taking the next steps on your journey. With each step you will receive a Gift. Each Gift will provide you with the means of connecting and staying connected to your True Self. There are 20 Gifts. Gifts you can use to create the relationships and life that you want. The Gifts will allow you to have your True Self truly reflected in the world, free from addiction.

Are you ready to Experience the Shift?

Your Next Step!

In the Magical Place of Awareness, you had your journal and special pen with you. You opened it and wrote down all of your thoughts and emotions. Much insights were gained. Now, you can have the actual journal in your hands. You can use it to learn more about yourself and to apply the *SHIFT* Principles in your life each and every day!

Now is the time.
This is the moment to create your Authentic Path.
For your own personal journal, go to
BonnieBarness.com

As you continue to move forward on your new path, connecting more and more with the source of your power to create and manifest your dreams, your True Self , you will gain specific Manifesting Principles in the Magical Place of Awareness and Nine Manifesting Charms. This knowledge is here for you right now! Are you ready to live in passion? Now is the time to choose the book or journal that resonates with your True Self. Know that I am by your side as you take the next step towards manifesting your dream!

TITLES BY THE Same Author

Coming Soon:

Manifesting Your Dreams: Experiencing the Shift

Emotional Intelligence

Esoteric Wisdom

Revealing YOU: Healing and Releasing Pain

Releasing Alcohol: Manifesting Your Dreams Journal

Releasing Drugs: Manifesting Your Dreams Journal

Releasing Weight: Manifesting Your Dreams Journal

BONNIE BARNESS

To be kept up to date with details of new releases and upcoming events, please sign-up for my mailing list.
Looking forward to your joining us soon!

Website:
BonnieBarness.com

Facebook:
Bonnie Barness, M.Ed.

YouTube:
Bonnie Barness
Connecting With Your True Self

CHOOSE YOUR
Thoughts

SHIFT YOUR
Feelings

CREATE YOUR
Dreams

BONNIE BARNESS

MADE IN THE USA
SCOTTSDALE, ARIZONA
FEBRUARY 2024

www.ingramcontent.com/pod-product-compliance
Lightning Source LLC
Chambersburg PA
CBHW051948290426
44110CB00015B/2152